# Choose
## Surthrival!

Are you ready to go from surviving
to thriving with a 21$^{st}$ Century
home-based business?

## Kim Power Stilson
*. . . talk radio host, eMedia Strategist & Power Mom who
has helped thousands promote themselves online!*

# DEDICATION

*To my parents, who gave me a world of history to be proud of.
My mother who opened the door to God, and my father who gave
me the branch of an Irish blackthorn tree to lean on as I need.*

# CONTENTS

# ACKNOWLEDGMENTS

Gratitude to the dogs at my feet, the birds at the sill, and the angels at my shoulder who keep me warm, happy, and inspired through seasons of radio and writing.

Thanks to . . . Jana Belliston, Diana Hoffman, Nina Isaacson, Kristen Lamb, Carla Russell, Carol Fredericks and Harriet Peterson for their lovely faces and compassionate service; Tom Egan who shared hope and instruction; Mark Crockett whose mission inspired me; David Ryan, the Power's in Dunmore East and Kim Power for being grand; Dave, Cheryl and family for their acceptance and timely assistance; Geoffrey, Evelyn, Dennis, Charles and Catherine for being lovely and fun siblings.

Appreciation and love most of all to the Three M's (Madelyne, McKall, Merrick) for their love and enormous faith in me, and of course, my handsome hero husband, Chad, for his strength.

Appreciation most of all to God, who loves me enough to keep the windows of Heaven open.

# ARE YOU SURVIVING OR THRIVING?

*"My mission in life is not merely to survive, but to thrive; and to do so with some passion, some compassion, some humor, and some style"*

**—Maya Angelou**

I lost my job at the same time I found I was pregnant with my first baby. I was 28. Having had a successful career to that point, I sent round resumes and thankfully found I was in demand. Within months I was on my fifth and final interview with a well-known company. The executive interviewing me noticed my expanded stomach and said, "It looks like you are pregnant!" She watched my face to confirm her suspicion, then continued, "How wonderful, what do you plan to do with the baby while you work?"

Usually well-prepared for interview questions I was hadn't expected that one, and blurted, "Are you even allowed to ask me that?" She gave me an innocent smile and said, "I am asking as a woman, not your potential boss. As you have chosen to be a mother, have you considered that your executive days may be over? How can a company team depend on someone who is partially focused on having a baby? If you need to work perhaps you would be better suited to a home-based business. "

I was offended. I had worked in big cities like New York, Tokyo, Los Angeles, how dare she suggest a home-based business to a savvy corporate executive like me? I told her what I thought of her suggestion on the spot. Not only did I not get that position, I was not offered any of the jobs I interviewed for until after my sweet baby was born and the appearance of the pregnancy faded.

When I went back to the corporate workplace as a new mother it was harder than I thought to balance my corporate aspirations with my family goals. Over the years I suffered as I left my babies behind with nannies while out of town on business or worked late through school activities. I went from the thriving in my career to barely keeping balance as a working mother. Finally after years of fighting to disprove that interview executive's theory, that I was more suited to a home-based business, I realized that she was actually absolutely right. Simply surviving from family to work and back, was not enough. Once I started a home-based business it wasn't long before my family and I began to thrive. For us the amount of effort it took to go from surviving to thriving was not difficult and the difference it makes in our lives is powerful.

The popularity of having a home-based business has gained credibility over the years since the idea was first recognized in 1978 as a viable industry option for American families. Home-based businesses can now easily compete with bigger businesses thanks to internet connections, smart phones, and 21$^{st}$ Century eMedia. Gone are the days when home-based businesses were exclusively run by shopkeepers who sold on the first floor while their families lived on the second floor. Now not only mothers but fathers and families are attracted to the convenient and lucrative possibilities of a home-based business.

For me having a home-based business has meant more money, and also sometimes more worry about money. It has meant less security yet more independence. Before the dot com bubble burst it was nice to have a regular paycheck but there had always been the fear that investors would stop the funding or the technology wouldn't work, and I'd once again be sending out resumes. Since owning my own business I have had spells with no income but at least no one could fire me but myself. It was nice to have a company help pay for my health insurance but overall having a home-based business has meant less stress, less Dr. visits and less medical costs.

At times I miss having a football-sized team of professionals to assist on projects but now my family has become my team. My kids know how to answer a phone call from an editor, do social media support, and set up for events. My daughters have helped me with events from high-profile Hollywood celebrity fund raisers to community parades, and national political events. My husband can engineer a radio show and set up website training better and faster than any staff member I've ever had. I don't have to wait on others to finish projects that stand in the way of an initiatives success, I can do them myself. I have become more talented, more practical, more creative and more resourceful and therefore much more valuable.

As the owner of my own home-based business, Power Strategies, Inc., I have had more money and time to enjoy life, serve others and just be with my family. I have more than a home-based business I have a better style of life and I love the freedom that comes from being able to say no or yes based on my own goals. I live on my own terms to fulfill my life's passion. Sure, with my Fame and promotions business I travel to Radio and TV broadcasts, Hollywood galas and fundraisers, meetings all over the nation and the occasional conference in Europe but afterwards I happily return home to my office, change from the glamorous business suit to do most of my work in my PJ's with my dogs snoring at my feet and my family nearby. I have not only survived I have learned to thrive with a little passion, compassion and style. I call that style Surthrival . . . and it's the perfect term for someone who has chosen to get beyond surviving to the vastly improved prospect of thriving.

Hundreds of people have asked me how I do it and if I think they could do it too and the answer to that question is why I wrote this book and called it *Choose Surthrival!*

If you are thinking about starting a business, the following questions and corresponding assignments may help you on your quest to thrive with 21st Century home-based business success!

# CHAPTER 1

# LOOKING FOR DIAMONDS?
## *Find Your Treasure at Home*

*"Diamonds may have been a girl's best friend in an era when a woman's only hope of having a high family income was to marry a man who was well off, but today, marketable skills that will enable a woman to command a good income over her lifetime are a better investment."*

—GRACE BARUCH

Did you know that there are enough diamonds in the world that if you distributed them evenly, every man, woman, and child would have their own cupful? Did you know that right now, you could have more than a cupful of diamonds worth of success by starting a business from your home? Since the world began, this time most favors home-based business. Sparkling solutions are available all around us if we open our minds and face our fears. Let me illustrate with a famous old story.

In 1861, Dr. Russell H. Conwell, author, minister, and an American Civil War soldier, first gave an address to a group of businessmen that has since been told and retold, printed and reprinted in the millions.

His address, "Acres of Diamonds," tells the story of a man named Ali Hafed who was told by a priest that diamonds were actually congealed drops of sunlight. Hafed decided that he wanted to own an entire mine of sunlight drops. He left his prosperous family farm and spent his life looking for diamonds. He never found them, never saw his family again, lost the family farm, and died. Years later, the new owner of Hafed's farm discovered a congealed drop of sunlight in his pasture. Ultimately that congealed drop of sunlight led to acres of diamonds mined from Hafed's old fields. Millions of dollars in diamonds were in Hafed's home pasture while he spent his life searching elsewhere.

Conwell's address suggests there are resources all around us. Had he been alive in the days of e-media I think he would have been more positive about his message. Today, e-media and the Internet provide solutions not unlike congealed drops of sunlight or diamonds, and they are there for the taking! E-media makes life easier, faster, greener, and less expensive. The Internet has leveled the playing field making all that was out of reach possible by learning home- based business success pointers.

Learning to use e-media is the key, and it doesn't have to be difficult to turn. Even a grandmother can learn to use new technology—mine did! My grandma grew up cooking large meals for farm hands on a firewood stove. Much later in life, when she found herself cooking for one, a friend suggested a microwave oven. My grandmother was overwhelmed and almost fearful of this new technology until I showed her how easy it was to melt rock-hard cheese to bubbles in seconds. After a few pointers, she could not remember how she had ever cooked without it.

In our rapidly changing world and new economy, many of may feel overwhelmed or inadequate. Times have changed, and the jobs we trained for may not be the jobs offered. When you hear of professionals with PhDs accepting jobs to sweep floors at night to avoid living on the streets, it's hard not to worry, but there is promise for us even today in today's economy.

During the Great Depression, when men left families behind to find work, women didn't let their families starve. They started collective groups that went from community to community in old school buses and wagons, trading carrots for quilts, apples for dental work, haircuts and hairdos for dinner. They created new industries from what they had to offer.

Historically, people always find solutions, and those solutions don't mean just surviving, they mean thriving! Some of the greatest money-making industries such as movie theaters and hair salons grew out of people searching for ways to feed their families when their source of income changed.

Going from a traditional business perspective to an e-media perspective, where you can build a thriving business from home, is like going from cooking for farm hands on a wood range to using a microwave. With a lesson or two, you will wonder how you ever worked without it.

Right now is the easiest and least expensive time in the history of the world to make money, become famous, and achieve success, all from home, thanks to e-media. If you are thinking about starting a business or have a business, the difference between success and thriving may reside in knowing your answers to the eleven questions in this book. You never know what will happen after you read this. I have high hopes that you will find acres of diamonds in your quest to make money from home and achieve twenty-first century style home-based business success!

## Question One: Are You Looking for Diamonds?

Before you search the world for answers it might be a good time just to check to see what valuable assets you have at home. For this first question assess your resources. Take a look around your home? What and who do you have of value? What resources and skills are close at hand? What hobbies do you have that could become a business? Who do you have around as a resource? Is what you most want nearer to hand than you think? Ask your family members the same questions and compare answers. Identify the treasures you have at home and keep them in mind as you read the rest of the questions.

# CHAPTER 2

# WHAT DO YOU WANT?
*The Power of Making Your Own Money*

*"Money never starts an idea; it is the idea that starts the money."*

—*W. J. Cameron*

What do you really want? Power, fame, money, love, or peace on earth? All of the above?

Let's say that you had an extra $90,000. Even better, let's say that all your basic bills and necessities are taken care of, you have everything you and your family could ever need, and you have an extra $90,000 to buy something special that you really want. How would you spend your money? Be honest and not especially altruistic here—what would you buy?

I pose this question in my e-media classes. Some people shout out the names of sport cars and dream vacations. Some answer that they would purchase helpful gifts for family members. Some students say that they would put their money in the bank for the future. Some students remain silent. I am never surprised to hear that some people have never thought of having more money than they need to survive. Some people don't dream beyond the next day, the next dollar, or the next leg of survival. To some, the idea that they could have an extra $90,000, or any kind of abundance, is a foreign concept. To be successful, you must think beyond survival and believe that abundance applies to you and your family. The most successful people believe that abundance comes from what they create, provide, and offer. Ask yourself what you really want, and the answer will let you know if you are heading the right direction.

## Question Two: What Do You Really Want?

Think about what you would buy if you had the extra $90,000! Really think about it, and choose something *you* would like—something selfish, something fun, something crazy, something that motivates you. It can be anything.

Now write it down. Where would you buy it? What does it feel, smell, and look like?

Get the visual of what you have decided to buy on paper and firmly set in your mind. Now let's go an extra step, talk about where you got the $90,000, and find out if the source of the funds makes a difference in how you would spend it.

**Boss.** Let's say that you got your money from your boss, who handed you $90,000 as a bonus. Would you feel that there must be strings attached? What would you buy?

**Finders keepers.** Let's say you found the $90,000 in the gutter, and you turned it into the police, but no one claimed it. What would you buy? Is this different from receiving the money from your boss?

**Mom.** Let's say your mom gave you $90,000. She just felt like handing over some cash to her kid. What would you buy? Is this different?

**Magic genie.** Let's say that, like Aladdin, you found a lamp, and a magic genie gave you not three wishes but $90,000. What would you buy? Is this different?

**Paying yourself through business success.** Let's say that you start a small business, pay all your bills, take care of your family, give to charity, pay the taxes and employees, and have $90,000 left over. What would you buy? Is this different?

Now think about the source you would rather accept the money from: your boss, finding it, your mom, the magic genie, or paying yourself through business success.

Which would you feel best about? Most fulfilled? Most excited, happy, pleased, and content? Which source would bring you the most joy? Write it down!

**First choice?**

**Why?**

**Second choice?**

**Why?**


**Third choice?**

**Why?**


Most people say that getting the money from business success is the most fulfilling, but then again, no one refuses a magic genie. If your first or second choice is paying yourself through stay-at-home business success, most likely you are or would be a great business owner.

If you agree that there is something appealing in the power of making your own money, you will want to keep reading.

# CHAPTER 3

# IS THIS THE RIGHT TIME?

*It's Not Your Grandparent's Great Depression*

*"Would you like me to give you a formula for success? It's quite simple, really. Double your rate of failure. You are thinking of failure as the enemy of success. But it isn't at all. You can be discouraged by failure or you can learn from it, so go ahead and make mistakes. Make all you can. Because remember that's where you will find success."*

—THOMAS J. WATSON

More people became millionaires during the Great Depression than at any other time in history. Opportunities that were not present during the boom times suddenly became available, proving that an economic downturn is a good time to consider starting a business. The great entrepreneur spirit of "if you can dream it, you can do it" helped many people make the best of the crisis as they provided a service or product in a new market.

When life hands you lemons and you can't afford sugar, all you have is sour juice. To be successful, you need to know what your soul can survive. Is it a question of "How much sour can we take before we give up?" Or is it "Can we learn to adapt the sour into something sweeter?"

Adaptation is an essential tool that you can learn by looking back. I grew up hearing about the Great Depression and the world war that supposedly ended the suffering. As a child, I was reprimanded if I did not eat and appreciate everything on my plate. My aunties told about sharing one tin of beans with a small side of whale blubber for their one daily meal during World War II. They were quick to remind me not to waste anything, because the memory of having nothing was vividly painful fifty years later.

I remember my grandmother giving me the task of cutting the buttons off clothing before we ripped them into cleaning rags. I put the buttons into a tin that contained every button ever worn by anyone in our family. How many of us clip buttons before tossing out an old coat today?

Adapting can also mean changing where we live and how we make money. My uncles used to tell stories of friends leaving their homes and families back east to find income picking strawberries and oranges in California. Some of those who left sent money back to their families and eventually returned home, and some were never heard from again. Many people moved their families and homes when the opportunity for work also became an opportunity for a better life.

My mother-in-law Cheryl's family lived in Wisconsin for many years until her grandfather moved to Arizona to find work in construction. He returned to Wisconsin after he made some money, but he missed the sunshine and the success of Phoenix so much that he returned with his family to live there permanently.

My uncles and aunts, grandmothers, and grandfathers knew firsthand how to adapt. People on both sides of my family immigrated to the United States from Northern Europe. One set survived the Great Depression, and the other survived World War II in England. Their stories formed my perception of what people will do when they want to survive.

My father's mother died of pneumonia, just after my father was born during World War II, in one of the most heavily bombed cities, Coventry, England. My granddad spent his time working in a Jaguar factory and in the pub, so my father was raised by his aunties. When my granddad remarried and new children came along, my father, who was by then a teenager, decided to live with family members who had immigrated to Bellflower, California.

My father arrived in California and slept on his aunt and uncle's pool table in the garage while he finished high school. My father said that he was one of the first to hear Johnny Cash play publicly and that he got into all kinds of trouble, racing cars and skipping school. He met my mom when my aunt sent him to borrow a cup of sugar from the house across the street. Marriage to my mom partially cured his wild streak, as together they had six children.

As a child, I crossed to one side of the street or the other to visit both sides of the family: Aunt Kit and Uncle Len on one side, my grandmother and grandpa on the other. In one house, I heard stories of surviving the Great Depression, and on the other side of the street, surviving World War II.

> *If you can't work with a broken back, move to where you can!*

The story of my mother's family emigrating from Scandinavia to Minnesota and then to California is particularly poignant. My grandparents were starting to do well on their farm in Minnesota when my grandfather broke his back and could no longer work. My grandmother heard that there were jobs in Southern California, and just like that, they had to make to make a tough decision: starve on the farm or try the unknown. Their dilemma was how they would get seven children and my grandfather, who was flat on his back in a cast, to California.

They came up with the idea of converting an old school bus into a makeshift motorhome. With only enough money for gas, all nine of them said goodbye and journeyed to California. My mother, who was a little girl at the time, remembers the trip as fun. My grandmother says that they were hungry and careworn but glad to arrive until they realized that they would all have to live in her cousin's tiny house. I shudder to think of nine people, including my five strapping teenage uncles, squeezing into a nine-hundred-square-foot, one-bathroom home in Bellflower.

According to the stories from all seven siblings, aside from fighting over the bathroom, they were so grateful to be in California that they didn't mind the lack of space. Jobs abounded, and when my grandpa's back healed, he got a job with McDonnell Douglas. My uncles say that they were pleased to have a career choice aside from farming, and it worked well for them. One became a fire chief, another a professor, and others entrepreneurs. Because they could not change their circumstances, they adapted and moved to a place where they lived successfully. My uncles and aunts all found jobs, careers, or businesses, and they still tell the story of the chance they took when they traveled cross country in a converted school bus.

*Had enough of the war?*
*Move to California!*

On the other side of the street, my Aunt Kit and Uncle Len told of stories of their families emigrating from England to the United States after the war. (Most of the stories were told in the evening after they had had a few drinks. My usually stoic Uncle

Len shared war-life stories which were darker and more graphic than I will share in this guide.) Some stories of the way the adapted to life changes on a daily basis during the war made me wish that I had never complained about anything.

Uncle Len told me once that during the darkest part of the war, my Uncle Fred got up in the morning after a terrible night of bombing, went to pick up his mate for school, and found his friend's home and others burned-out. On his way to school he had to step over the lifeless forms of friends and their mothers. Uncle Len said he, my Uncle Fred, and the other school kids sifted through the cinders to find toys and treasures and keep them in honor of their fallen school mates. Some of my family members still have boxes of treasures that even fifty years later they look at and say, "Look at this, this is Johnny's best tin soldier." I asked once why they were so disrespectful of the dead, picking through the rubble to find their belongings. My Uncle Fred said, "Johnny would have done the same of me. Things were scarce then, you wouldn't understand." He was right, I didn't understand, but the look in his eyes told me that his memories were painful.

By the end of World War II, Uncle Len was finally old enough to join the war effort. He said that the bombing had ruined most of his favorite fishing spots and that more than anything else made him want to fight back. He played the trumpet the military band to give relief to troops and served his time on a clean-up detail in Germany after the war. It is rumored to this day that his family had Hitler's letter opener, acquired when Uncle Len swept through on special duty with the Allies.

My Uncle Len said that adapting to the war saved his life. On a night, when he was assigned to play a big gig for the troops in London, he arrived late at his assigned hotel and was told that there were no rooms left. The hotel he was reassigned to was not as fancy or close to town, and Uncle Len was understandably disappointed. In a foul temper, he played the gig that night, and while his troop spent the night in luxury, he traveled alone back to his old hotel. Luxury then was not it is now; to Uncle Len, luxury was a spoon of jam with breakfast. He said that back then he would have given most anything for a spoonful of jam. During the night, air raid sirens wailed, and Uncle Len came out of the hotel shelter the next morning to find the luxurious hotel he would have stayed in burned to the ground with his buddies in it. Right then, he decided to accept the situations life handed him with more appreciation.

After all Len had been through as a young soldier, he grabbed at the chance to move to the United States a few years after the war. He married my Aunt Kit, moved to California, and bought a house with a pool. He described California to his family back in England saying, "Orange groves and strawberry fields as far as the eye can see, plenty of fishing holes, and all the jam I want." These words eventually persuaded my teenage father to take a boat ride alone from England and join them. Uncle Len started a reupholstering business, played trumpet in a local band, and lived to a ripe old age while smoking like a chimney. He was successful financially, but most importantly, he loved life and appreciated it. He always missed England; you could tell. As soon as he heard the strains of "Rule Britannia," he was on his feet, tears in his eyes, shouting, "God Save the Queen!"

> ### *It's our turn—what are we willing to do?*

When I came to him with a skinned knee, Uncle Len said, "Trials lead to success if you know how to look at them!" He then shared a quote from Winston Churchill, one that had given him and his countrymen the courage to persevere: "Do not speak of darker days; let us speak rather of sterner days. These are not dark days; these are great days—the greatest day our country has ever lived, and we must all thank God that we have been allowed each of us according to our stations, to play a part in making these days memorable in the history of our race."

The people in our past are not to be forgotten. They have left us a legacy of survival and adapting to dire circumstances. To me, they are examples of the grandest of humankind, the kind that faces unimaginable horror and looks for the best in life.

Is this the right time? Was there ever a right time? Whatever you are experiencing now, no matter how tough times are, a look at the devastating odds that people have survived and how they adapted will balance your perspective. Those who lived before you faced challenges as stiff as those you face today, and they not only survived, they succeeded. If they overcame their challenges by adapting to life's "lemons," it stands to reason that you can too. If you have or are thinking about creating your own business to adapt to life's challenges, history will show you how success is not only possible but highly probable. Find out if it's the right time by answering Question Three.

## Question Three: Is This the Right Time?

Talk with three business owners; asking them about their successes and failures to help you determine if this is the right time for you to start or grow your own business.

Ask them what has most helped them succeed, what advice they can share, and how to choose the right time to start a business. Offer to take your interviewee to lunch or make a quick phone appointment. Choose your people, interview them, write down the answers, and compare.

Here are some examples of questions; feel free to add your own.

- Can you share an example of failing?

- Can you share an example of overcoming a failure?

- Was the failure worth the eventual success?

- What has helped you succeed?

- Looking back, what would you not do again?

- What advice would you share?

- When is the best time to start a business?

- Did you ever want to quit?

- How do you keep going? What motivates you?

- Do you love what you do?

## Business Owner(s)
## Name, Business, Years in Business

Once you have completed the interviews, take a look at the answers. Did you find that there is a right time to start a business? Was the agony of failure worth the eventual success?

If you felt inspired by the answers you found, you may be ready to *Choose Surthrival* with a twenty-first-century home-based business!

## CHAPTER 4

# CAN YOU PUT YOUR OXYGEN MASK ON FIRST?

*Taking Care of Your Greatest Asset*

*"Most people work harder for strangers than they do for themselves."*

—STEPHEN V. RICHARDSON

Who cares more about your ambitions, passions, hopes, dreams, health, and business than you? The power of making your own money comes from your company's greatest asset: you. If your company's product was diamonds, you'd keep them safe in a vault. If your company trained horses, you would take impeccable care of them. If your company hosted websites, you would have a reliable server. Smart business owners take precious care of their goods or hire someone they trust to do it, but how well do the business owners take care of themselves?

As the greatest asset of a home-based business, it is imperative that you prioritize your own well-being.

You may have been on a plane or seen the movies where the flight attendant reminds you to put on your oxygen mask first before assisting others. You know the reason for that: if you aren't breathing, how can you help others? As simple as it sounds, putting your oxygen mask on first applies to your business too.

> *"Healthcare costs are nearly 50% greater for workers who report high levels of stress."*
>
> —*"CONTROL YOUR STRESS" ARTICLE ON MEREDITH .COM*

If you are considering starting a business, the reality is that you will be doing everything yourself: accounting, collections, selling, marketing, fulfillment, maintenance, and customer service, as well as all that you do to make your product or service unique.

Doing everything yourself can be stressful, and that is why having a small business is not for the faint of heart. Sure, you set your own hours and are your own boss, but if you have an ambitious bone in your body, you will be your toughest boss ever.

When you work full-time for someone else, you are making that person rich, but do you take vacation days or sick days? Some are lucky enough to get 401(k) benefits, healthcare benefits, or tuition reimbursement. Smart employers know that they have to take care of their employees; without employees, the company ceases to thrive. Smart business owners know this and appreciate their workers.

More than seven million small businesses are started every year in the United States alone, and if you want a chance at success, start your venture right or make the corrections now to take care of your company's greatest asset: *you*.

It may be surprising that taking care of yourself is among the first questions here, but if you can answer the question positively, you will be successful. Why? You will have endurance. If you never quit, you will never fail. Many new small-business owners experience health-related issues that slow them down or stop them within the first three years. If you take care of yourself, you will not have that issue.

> *"It is a shameful thing for the soul to faint while the body still perseveres."*
>
> —*Marcus Aurelius*

In a related vein, physical breakdown isn't the only health issue that small business owners face. Let's look at some of the issues you should consider when thinking about starting or continuing your small business.

You'll find below a list of suggestions to help you help your business by taking care of yourself first. Each suggestion includes a brief explanation. When you have the time, I suggest that you read *The 4-Hour Workweek* by Timothy Ferriss. I read it during a camping trip, and it finally dawned on me how important it is to live a life that I enjoy. I turned my life around. Though I work more than four hours a week (about thirty-five hours a week, down from more than seventy), I enjoy my stay-at-home work life more without sacrificing success!

Let's start with the following suggestions:

Determine what sets you off

Accept what you can't control

Pay yourself first

Consider TV

Get three hobbies

Smell the flowers

Use the highest quality fuel

Adjust your attitude

Laugh a lot

Add music

Pet your pet

Shower the people you love with love

Don't envy the competition

Adapt with flexibility

Appreciation

Take time to recoup

Frequent service

E-media exercise

## Determine what sets you off

What makes you irritable or angry? Negative reactions to situations are indicators that something is not right with you. Someone driving recklessly is unforgivable and would worry anyone, but the way you react to that event indicates how well you are.

Here are some common emotional reactions to business stress. I listed the situations that gave me a specific emotional reaction and then the physical symptoms I experienced.

**Mad**

1. I get mad when my team repeatedly misses deadlines.

2. I get mad when people talk on their cellphone and don't pay attention.

3. I get mad when the Internet is slow.

**What physical symptoms do you experience when this happens?**

A vein in my head throbs.

## Angry

1. I get angry when people say they will do something and then don't.

2. I get angry when just as I'm making a point, the phone rings, the person answers it, and the moment is lost.

## What physical symptoms do you experience when this happens?

My chest gets tight.

There are several more examples and an exercise at the end of this chapter. Now that the above has helped identify what sets me off, I will describe what makes me feel great and happy in common business situations.

Below I have listed the situations that make me feel that emotion and then added the physical symptoms that I experienced.

## Energetic

1. I feel energetic when everything falls into place.

2. I am energized when I sell.

3. I feel energetic when I have a challenge that I know I can overcome.

## What physical symptoms do you experience when this happens?

I feel light and enthusiastic!

**Positive**
I feel positive when my team works together.

**What physical symptoms do you experience when this happens?**

I feel alive and like I can accomplish anything.

Read the lists again. Do you notice anything interesting? After the first set, most people see that the negative emotions manifest in specific parts of their body (headache, stomachache, etc.).

On the other hand, with the second set, the positive emotions seem to be an overall, body-wide feeling. Some people write "great" for every reaction. I've noticed this in myself.

Most of the time, we let situations and how we perceive them determine our emotions. We need stress or we would be dead, but keeping track of how you react to situations and then *choosing* your reaction is a smart way to keep that "oxygen mask" on.

> *Accept what you can't control*

A plaque hanging on a wall at my grandmother's house reads as follows.

*"God grant me the serenity to accept the things I cannot change, courage to change the things I can, and the wisdom to know the difference."*

—*"THE SERENITY PRAYER" BY REINHOLD NIEBUHR*

I remember this when I try to control the outcome of a situation. No matter what you say, do, or wish, you cannot change what other people decide to do. You can try, but ultimately the decision is theirs. Respect that, and let go of control. When I feel myself getting tense, I repeat the proverb in my mind.

If the situation is too tense for this proverb, I go with this one (I used it while fighting with a rental car guy on our last family trip to Ireland):

*"Patience is a bitter cup from which only the strong can drink."*

—*GEORGE BERNARD SHAW*

My kids can repeat this quote verbatim because I use it so much. Some people suggest counting to ten when you feel impatient in a situation that you can't control, but my mind is too active to be pacified easily. Pick a quote that calms your nerves and won't be offensive if you repeat it out loud. Although I can't control a situation, I can influence it. More often than not, a proverb or quote has brought empathy and amusement from the other person and sometimes turns the situation in my favor.

## Pay yourself first

My husband's aunt, Elva, does our taxes. She advocates paying ourselves first—10 percent of what we make. My husband and I believe in tithing 10 percent to our church, so we do that too. Paying yourself can be rewarding, so no matter how poor I feel, I do it even when I only make a few hundred bucks. Why not? Ten percent to God and ten percent to me seems fair to me.

For small businesses, paydays can be few and far between in the beginning, so think about how to pay yourself in ways that reward your efforts from the beginning.

## Consider TV

My mother used to say, "Television isn't all bad in moderation. Just don't sit too close, or you'll lose your eyesight!" I think that TV can be a great source of entertainment for those on a budget. Pick a few shows to record, and treat yourself during the week. Fast-forward through the commercials, and watch your shows as you would a movie—sit down with popcorn, soy chips, celery stalks, or my favorite, chocolate, and enjoy the show! A little laughter, drama, or escape from reality never hurt anyone and will give you a much-needed break.

## *Get three hobbies*

Winston Churchill, a busy leader during a time of great crisis, said that having three hobbies that had nothing to do with his main focus or livelihood helped him be successful. Having time for three hobbies sounds challenging, but think of the plus side: more opportunity to become good at something besides what you are already good at. One of Churchill's hobbies was painting watercolors of his friends' gardens.

During a particularly stressful time in my life, a friend suggested taking up a hobby. I could not think of a hobby that I wanted to do—one that would take me away from the computer—except for painting. I found a watercolor set that my husband had given me two Christmases before and sat in my garden. As I sat there trying to get inspired, I noticed all the weeds in my garden and soon was digging in the dirt. It wasn't until winter came and the weeds were buried under snow that I started painting, and then I painted bluebirds on spring flowers. My garden and my paintings are not show quality, but they get me away from the computer, and I am surprised at what a wonderful holiday they offer when I don't have time for a real vacation.

My husband is an emergency first responder with our local fire department, and he enjoys archery and studies Russian. His hobbies give him a break from the stress of his job.

What would you like to do? Even if you love what you do for a living, giving yourself an entirely separate hobby is a great way to pay yourself back for your hard work.

## Smell the flowers

A talented technical wizard I once worked with had this quote on his desk: "If you get simple beauty and naught else, you get about the best thing God invents."

Each day, he took a walk around the building, and I could see him sniffing the flowers or picking up handfuls of snow, as the season dictated. He took time to appreciate the little things for a moment and then got back to work. He was hailed by some of the largest companies in the world as an innovative genius.

I work in a home in the mountains surrounded by trees, flowers, and weeds. I often see deer from my window and watch as robins pounce in the trees during their spring worm feast. I take time every day to appreciate the simple beauty that God delivers right to my doorstep.

## Use the highest quality fuel

When I worked full time, what do you think was the most common item I found on every person's desk? Stapler? A Phone? A Big Gulp® A friend of mine used to say, "My inventions are fueled by Dr. Pepper®!" That good friend is now in her forties and has diabetes. What you throw into your body every day is as important as any other choice you make. If you cut out caffeine and alcohol and find other ways to stimulate (and de-stress) your body, you will be healthier. Have you ever counted the number of sodas or cups of coffee or chocolate bars you have eaten in a month just to "keep going"?

Keep a bowl of frozen berries or a bag of carrots by your desk. If you work at home, set a timer and get up, drink some water, and get a sandwich or snack every two hours. I have a friend who used to sit at a computer all day and eat whatever was handy or fast. Her desk was littered with burrito wrappers, soda cups, and chip bags. Her work was suffering the last time I saw her, and then she lost a ton of weight and was making a ton of money. She went from being overweight and poor to successful and healthy in a few months. Someone advised her that she could eat all the junk she wanted if she first ate her daily servings of fruits and veggies. Now, before she turns on her computer each day, she puts out veggies and fruit and eats those before the pizza, chips, chocolate, soda, coffee, or meat. She swore that she would never give up junk food, and she hasn't, but she says that eating all those veggies seemed to give her brain the fuel she needed to finish a project she had been fiddling with for years. That project brought her a year's worth of salary in one week. She now swears that she will never give up veggies and fruit!

I was reminded of her story while writing this, so in the last three days, I tried it myself. I have lost four pounds eating veggie soup and fresh fruit first before eating "real food," as my son calls it. It was easier than officially dieting, and I feel great.

## *Adjust your attitude*

I am a big believer in the adage, "When life gives you lemons, make lemonade." The first time I heard this was when I was eleven, and my grandpa had just died. I was crying because he could not dance with me at my wedding as he had promised. Someone (surely sick of my whining) made the lemonade statement. It did not make sense to me; how could there be anything positive about my grandfather dying? How could I make anything sweet out of something so sour?

On my radio show, I shared this story with my listeners. A man said, "You need to adjust your attitude!" He said that he lost his leg in World War II, lost his wife and child in a car accident, and had still managed to "make lemonade." He was the administrator in a boy's home. He said that life is like sour lemon juice and "adding sugar" is like adjusting your attitude and making the best of whatever life hands you. His work did not take away the pain he had suffered but made it sweeter and easier to swallow. What humbling, powerful advice!

## *Laugh a lot!*

*"A well-developed sense of humor is the pole that adds balance to your steps as you walk the tightrope of life."*

—WILLIAM ARTHUR WARD

My friend, Brent Sims, is a funny guy. I have known him since we attended early-morning seminary classes at our church during our high school years. Brent has that kind of sarcastic humor that makes you laugh not only as he says something but again a few hours later when you think about it.

These days, Brent is a handsome attorney with a wonderful family, yet when I think of him, I see him as he was as he was a kid when he rarely wore shoes. In any weather, we found him barefoot and cracking jokes with friends. Our seminary classes started at six in the morning and even on the cold days, he did not wear shoes. The teachers got after him to "put some shoes on!" and he respectfully cracked a joke. No matter what he said in response, the teachers always laughed.

I thought of him as a brave nonconformist for not wearing shoes. Now I think it wasn't so much that he was rebellious but that he always did what made him comfortable. Not wearing shoes made him happy, and that allowed him to crack jokes that made us all laugh. I used to say that he would travel the world in bare feet, and I do know he went to Taiwan on a mission for the LDS church. I wondered if being in China gave him an advantage on his barefoot commitment.

I saw Brent last year, and he looked as young as he did in high school, if not a little more distinguished. I asked him if he had, as an attorney, taken to wearing shoes. He said that he wore them in court because they made him, but he never wore them at his desk if he could help it. Brent adopted a son from China who is always flipping off his shoes, so I guess his legacy will live on! I asked him the secret to why he was always laughing, and he said, "I can't help it. Everything tickles my feet!"

If you have or are thinking about starting your own business, surely you can use more laughter in your life. Aside from the fact that customers like to buy from people they like (and who is more popular than someone who is happy and fun?), we need to laugh to live another day. Find out what makes you laugh, and add more of it to your life. If you don't feel like laughing, take your shoes off while you sit at your desk. You may find that Brent is on the something!

*Pet your pet*

*Kim with her Irish Wolfhounds Daisy and Lucky.*

There is a reason over 83 million households have a pet or two. Pets have been shown to reduce blood pressure and decrease stress levels. Animals are happy to be feed, walked, groomed and loved . . . no other intricate instructions needed really for them to be happy members of the family. Just the act of petting the dog or cuddling with the cat can make you feel happier. There is lots of scientific proof for pets online but suffice to say that after the amount of dogs, cats, birds, snakes, guinea pigs and fish my family has loved I can attest to their value. My husband who gets tired of the chewing and messes may strongly disagree but if you look at my husband on any given evening there is a dog at his feet, a cat curled on his lap and usually a smile on his face.

### *Add Music*

When we were kids and our dad was building his business, we only saw him at night when he came home for a quick dinner. Before he could afford a security system, he slept in a chaise lounge at his office guarding the electronics that he refurbished for Panasonic and Yamaha. He ate and rushed off unless we could get him to sit down with a guitar. When he held a guitar in his hands, something magical happened, and we all sat around as a family and sang Johnny Cash and Willie Nelson songs. The stress seemed to melt from my dad's face. I see that now in my brother, Geoff, who swears he is nothing like my dad. (You know how fathers and sons can be.) Even when he is stressed, Geoff picks up a guitar, strums, and sings until he has forgotten his cares—for that moment, anyway.

Not ready to learn a new instrument right now? My friend said that the best investment she ever made in her small business was getting an iPod and loading it with her favorite and cheeriest songs. She said, "Even if you don't know how to use an iPod or iPad, get one, and fill it with your favorite songs. Someone will show you how. Stick the earphones in your ear if you ever doubt your ability to keep going. It works and may help you hang on a while longer on your path to success."

### *Shower the people you love with love*

Speaking of music, I am a big James Taylor fan; I go to all of his concerts that I can. My kids know the words to his songs though they are embarrassed to admit it. His song, "Shower the People You Love with Love" is great advice and timely. The tougher things are in business, the tougher things will be for your family and team members. Love them up a little. Hand out hugs, thank you cards, and appreciation. Shower them so much that they reach for their umbrella.

The middle sister, Evelyn Florence, named after both my grandmas, looks nothing like people must think when she gives her name over the phone. They must envision a sweet, tiny old-fashioned aunt with a plate of cookies. Evelyn is actually a tall, young, gorgeous strawberry blonde with a great smile! She is, however, great at making everyone feel loved, good at making each person she contacts feel special, which is an art. It is a God-given gift, and some like my sister Evie are lucky to have it!

Giving a little when life is tough is a form of service that gives back. Showing love is inexpensive and invaluable and never fails to light the road to happiness.

## *Don't envy the competition, compete*

St. Francis De Sales, a Roman Catholic Saint known for his writings on spiritual direction in 1620's wrote:

*"Do not wish to be anything but what you are, and try to be that perfectly!"*

—*St. Francis De Sales*

It is easy to look around and see people who are more successful than you. I once complained about this to my father-in-law, and he said that the surest way to fail is to envy the competition. Instead, compete with it. He says, "It's a good day when your competition succeeds! If they can, so can you! If they are doing well, get out there and compete for that business."

I read in an article by Napoleon Hill that if you look at people who have more, instead of being envious, think, "Good for them. I can have that too!" and go after it. Letting go of envy and focusing on the goal will give you more energy and a better chance for success!

## Adapt with flexibility

When you start a business, you never know where your journey will take you. Being flexible with your expectations will allow ease of movement when you need to change your strategy. A friend of mind started a lawn-mowing business in Orange County while he was in college. He was in business school and studying Japanese and wanted to work for a specific Japanese company when he graduated.

His lawn-mowing business was the most flexible business he could think, of so he started knocking on doors, asking people in prestigious parts of Newport Beach if he could mow their lawns. At the first house, the owner said, "I have that taken care of, but do you clean pools?" My buddy could have said that he only mowed lawns, but he said, "Sure, I do pools." He went home and studied pool cleaning before he went back the next day.

My friend did so well cleaning pools that eventually he hired his brothers and then his brother's friends to work for what is still one of the most successful pool-cleaning companies in Southern California. The best part is that through cleaning pools of prestigious homeowners, he met a top executive of the company he wanted to work for, and he found a job before he graduated from college doing exactly what he wanted. His brother continued the pool company, and as far as I know, my friend has never wanted financially, because he learned early the value of adapting.

## *Appreciation*

Appreciation is a big thing with me. More blessings, luck, providence, or whatever you want to call it have come to me because I took the time to express my appreciation.

I worked in Japan for a couple of years, and I noticed how many ways people express their appreciation to each other. I loved the culture of appreciation. Gifts are given generously and symbolically. Appreciation isn't just about gift-giving or saying thank you; it is more about recognizing the impact another person has on your life!

I devote an entire chapter to appreciation in my guide, *24 Hours to Zero-Down Marketing* (offered as Step One in the "Surthrival Series for Home-based Business Success.") Appreciation is an important practice to cultivate! Just saying "thank you" is not always enough. Amazing things happen when you take the time to appreciate people.

## Take time to recoup

*"If I stoop into a dark tremendous sea of cloud, it is but for a time. I press God's lamp close to my breast; its splendor, soon or later, will pierce the gloom; I shall emerge one day."*

—ROBERT BROWNING

The most successful business people will tell you that they experienced failure before they experienced success. Failure is not easy to swallow, but it is part of your journey if you are to be successful. When it happens, take time to recoup. Take an hour or a day to accept, understand, and assess what happened. Sometimes a tough day is losing a client or having my computer server die during a presentation. It could always be worse! When I start to feel that I can't face another problem or person, I leave my technology behind and go outside to swing in my hammock. Just me, the dogs, and the trees. I hide out for a while.

There is nothing wrong with taking a rest after you fail; all that matters is that you eventually emerge and get back on track for success.

## *Frequent service*

My husband and I were the first of our friends to be hit with what is now euphemistically referred to as the New Economy. Starting in 2006 with a series of clients who couldn't pay their invoices, the loss of major accounts, business contracts that never came to fruition, and partners quitting, we needed to find work. By 2009, we hadn't found jobs and were as poor as we had ever been. We were in the same position then as millions of people all over the world are now: well educated, well experienced, and needing work. Driving home from another depressing job interview, I was feeling sorry for myself when I noticed a sign reading "Need Work" being waved at the car in front of us.

I watched as the old and road-worn car ahead of us slowed to offer some money to the well-dressed family sitting on the corner. Witnessing that gracious act by someone who looked like he ought to keep his money had me identifying both with the family on the corner and the person in the old car. That day what I saw irrevocably shifted my perception and reminded me of a quote from over a hundred years ago.

*"When you find yourselves a little gloomy, look around you and find somebody that is in a worse plight than yourself; go the him and find out what the trouble is,*

*then try to remove it with the wisdom which the Lord bestows upon you; and the first thing you know, your gloom is gone, you feel light, the spirit of the Lord is upon you, and everything seems illuminated."*

—LORENZO SNOW, *LDS CONFERENCE REPORT, APRIL 6, 1899*

The promise of illumination in that quote opened my heart and changed my attitude. When you own a home-based business and do a lot of your work on the Internet, it's easy to focus on your own problems. It's a good idea to schedule time to serve. You might sit on the boards of nonprofit groups, get involved with your favorite causes, and volunteer in the community. Those service acts can be good for your community and your business, but it's also good for your soul to give back in little ways. Be open to helping those who are having a bad day, need some spare change, or need their sidewalk shoveled. There aren't many committee-run projects helping those who need a plate of cookies or a lift to the gas station. Who takes care of those folks? If you give back by giving in little ways, you will find great blessings in life.

I read this saying on a plaque in a neighbor's garden:

---

*"Through this toilsome world, alas, Once and only once I pass, If a good deed I may do, If an act of kindness I may show, Let me do it while I can, No delay for it is plain, I shall not pass this way again."*

---

## *E-media exercise*

Because my mission was to find stay-at-home success through twenty-first-century e-media, I would be remiss if I did not mention my Wii video game console. It's sad to say, but some days my Wii Fit Trainer is the only one telling me that I am doing a great job! I try to do thirty minutes of Wii Fit Yoga or games each day. Some days, I am walking a tightrope, sometimes I do boxing sessions, and some days I find myself staring at a flickering flame. My balance, attitude, and focus have improved since I added Wii time to my regular fitness routine.

If you are a bit of a home-office hermit, like me, you will find it easier to fit a Wii workout into your schedule than a trip to a gym. My balance, weight, tone, and flexibly have improved since I have had my own yoga fitness trainer at my beck and call. E-media exercise is a benefit of working from home in the twenty-first century.

### Question Four: Can You Put Your Oxygen Mask on First?

Find out how well you know yourself by trying the exercises you read about in the "Determine what sets you off" section. To answer this first question write down one to the  situations that set you off and then list the physical symptoms you experience. Take some time, and be honest; remember, no one will read this but you!

**What makes you Mad?**

1.

2.

3.

**What physical symptoms do you experience when this happens?**

1.

2.

3.

Now think about what makes you feel great, joyful, or happy. Write one to three situations that give you a specific reaction, and then list the physical symptoms you experience.

**What makes you feel great?**

1.

2.

3.

**What physical symptoms do you experience when this happens?**

1.

2.

3.

If you take the time to take care of your greatest asset and put your own mask on first, you may be ready to *Choose Surthrival* for twenty-first-century home-based business success!

# CHAPTER 5

# DO YOU ALREADY KNOW THE SECRET TO SURTHRIVAL?
### *Is Positive That Powerful?*

*"You must not allow yourselves to become discouraged. Work brings joy, optimism, and happiness. Don't give Satan an opportunity to discourage you. Here again, work is the answer. The Lord has given us a key by which we can overcome discouragement: Come unto me, all ye that labor and are heavy laden, and I will give you rest. Take my yoke upon you, and learn of me; for I am meek and lowly in heart; and ye shall find rest unto your souls. For my yoke is easy and my burden is light."*

—EZRA TAFT BENSON AND MATTHEW 11:28–30

Yes, being positive is powerful! There are a lot of ways to look at being positive. Some are more traditional, some are more popular, and you need to find what works for you.

Years ago while hosting the "Healthy Wealthy Wow" radio show, many of the guests referenced *The Secret*. When James Ray, a contributor to the movie and subsequently the book by Rhonda Byrnes, was to be interviewed on my show, I asked, "What is *The Secret?*"

Pam Montero, my next interview guest, heard my question and kindly lent me her copy of the book to prepare for the interview. I ended up reading it while bored on the cruise. (Yes, "bored" is what happens when workaholics go on a seven-day cruise and are bereft of phone, laptop and business communication.) It turned out that boredom was the best thing for me. If you go to thesecret.tv, you'll find this quote:

> "The Secret reveals the most powerful law in the universe. The knowledge of this law has run like a golden thread through the lives and the teachings of all the prophets, seers, sages and saviors in the world's history, and through the lives of all truly great men and women. All that they have ever accomplished or attained has been done in full accordance with this most powerful law. Without exception, every human being has the ability to transform any weakness or suffering into strength, power, perfect peace, health, and abundance."
>
> —*Rhonda Byrnes*

What I liked best about *The Secret* wasn't that while going through a tough time in her life, Byrne made a discovery through a one-hundred-year-old book that gave her the secret to prosperity, health, relationships, and happiness or, as she says, "The secret to life." That was great, but what I really liked was that when she found a solution to her problem, she did something about what she discovered. She took a chance; she created a film that has been viewed by millions of people around the world.

Byrne says, "*The Secret* reveals the natural law that is governing all lives. By applying the knowledge of this law, you can change every aspect of your life." You can tell that she believes it.

## *My experience with The Secret*

After reading the book, I was so encouraged that I made a vision board of what I wanted in my life. I pasted on it magazine cutouts of the things I wanted to accomplish: finally writing my book, working at home to be around my soon-to-be teenage kids, a luxurious red car I'd always wanted, regular trips to my family home in Ireland, breeding Irish Wolfhounds, and being an independent businesswoman.

I was so open to opportunities that, I subscribed to a multilevel (MLM) type of online shopping business that gave cash back for every person I referred. My goal was to have enough shoppers shopping every month to fund the life I wanted to live, the life I had displayed on my vision board.

This new business would give me regular income through an online source, so I would never be tied to my desk. I was excited so I got to work. The ideas in *The Secret* seemed to bring great success immediately. In a few months, I added almost two hundred shoppers to this business and made new friends who I encouraged to shoot for grand goals. Six months later, the MLM business failed, leaving me and our new crew of *The Secret* shoppers in the dust.

I took that failure to heart and stuffed my vision board behind a bunch of boxes.

Years later, I found the vision board and was surprised to find that I had accomplished half of the items on it. I had depicted finishing my book, *24 Hours to Zero-Down Marketing*—two years later I had done so. I was spending time with my kids because I now had a home-based business. There was a sweet red car in the garage, and we had just welcomed a litter of Irish Wolfhound puppies. Years later, some of the dreams I wanted came true, not in the way I originally planned through that other company but in a way that was much better: through my own business.

## *Failure—proof that The Secret works?*

After reading *The Secret* and planning to be attract what I wanted, I experienced many failures. It seemed that it wasn't enough to face the misery of rallying people to invest in a company that failed. Being of strong Northern European stock, I didn't give up easily, but no matter how hard I tried, I failed to achieve any success in business.

I had to face one failure after another. All were learning experiences, sure, but I like success. I was used to success, and *The Secret* seemed to have put me on a path to failure. I realize now that the path wasn't one of failure but of rearranging my life to obtain what I desired.

## *Beyond The Secret*

Dr. Lisa Love's book, *Beyond the Secret,* shares that you get what you focus on but that it isn't always what is best for you. I noticed the book in the garage, leftover from stacks of books submitted by publishers to my defunct radio show. I read it while spending a week at a beach cottage, during a time that I knew I was about to crack under the strain of all the failures. A quote on the back of the book by Larry Dossey, MD and author of *The Extraordinary Healing Power of Ordinary Things,* drew me in.

> *"The much ballyhooed Law of Attraction should come with a warning—Oscar Wilde's observation that 'When the gods want to punish us, they answer our prayers.' It is no secret that people attract what they want; the key is to want the right things, for the right reasons."*
>
> **—DR. LARRY DOSSEY**

In the book, Love shares a profound story about paying attention to what your Ego wants—new cars, beach houses, etc.—and what your Spirit wants: to do good, contribute, and feel fulfilled. I decided to try using the Law of Attraction as she suggested.

*"When you use the law of attraction, instead of focusing on what feels good, focus on what feels right. Feel good by doing good."*

She suggested focusing on a path that includes service as well as all the fun things you would like. This shifted my perspective; I believe that it prevented a personal breakdown and put me onto the path of a more peaceful kind of success.

Now on a shifted path, I saw how all the failures I experienced put me in the position to accomplish what I can in life.

While there is power in being positive about what you want, you can't control the outcome. Whatever the world wants to call it, I believe that our lives, no matter how perfectly planned, ultimately lie in the hands of God.

Focusing on that has taken me closer to real success than ever before. Being positive and hoping for the best while taking actions that are profoundly directed toward the positive has proved more advantageous than the life I used to lead.

If you have or are thinking about starting a home-based business, to be clear about what you want to achieve. When you are clear, you can face any failure and any success with faith.

## Question Five: Do You Already Know the Secret to Surthrival?

Take some time to think beyond surviving and what it would be like to thrive, really thrive and live well. What would each day be like if you were really living your life the way you wanted to? Consider the things you have always wanted to do perhaps, write a book, scuba dive, climb Mt. Everest, or learn a new language, and don't be hesitate to add that to your life's vision. Focus on seeing yourself the way you want to be living. Write all that in a journal, or make a vision board, or just outline it all visually in your head.

Need a little help to get started? You can learn Ann Webb's ideas on creating a life vision that includes your entire life, not just the part that makes money, at ideallifevision.com

Surviving is one thing most of us already do well. Taking steps to thrive well may simply be the difference of just a little extra focus.

# CHAPTER 6

# DO YOU HAVE ALL THREE SUCCESS COMPONENTS?

*Passion, Plan, Action*

*"Something in human nature causes us to start slacking off at our moment of greatest accomplishment. As you become successful, you will need a great deal of self-discipline not to lose your sense of balance, humility, and commitment."*

**—H. R. PEROT**

If you have or are thinking about starting a business, what's keeping you from doing it? Money? The economy? Time? What keeps people from success? Failure to act? Resignation? Are they thinking, "It's too late for me!" or "I've missed an opportunity, I don't have any great ideas"?

Laurel Delaney, the Founder of Globe Trade.com, says in "The World is Your Market: Small Business Gear Up For Globalization," many entrepreneurs think that going global is too complicated and confusing.

"Never before in the history of the world, has the entrepreneurial and small business spirit been more alive! The fight-for-your life attitude caused by extreme uncertain times along with the explosive growth of the Internet has leveled the playing field . . . there is no end in sight. Rather, a beginning to realizing the world is your market."

I think Delaney is right, and millions agree! (I suggest taking a look at her article at scribd.com for further value.) Only 10 percent of small businesses are involved in the global marketplace, according to her paper.

According to Dun & Bradstreet in an article entitled "Recession Brought a Small-Business Boom" published on Portfolio.com in May 2011, "Compared to 2007, there was a huge increase in the number of business failures in 2008, 2009, and 2010. In fact, the number of business failures in 2009 was almost twice that of the amount of failures in 2007," writes Byron Vielehr, president of global risk and analytics at D&B, in response to questions emailed by Portfolio. com. "However, 2009 and 2010 bore witness to the highest percentage of startups in more than a decade. The rate of new businesses had also been steadily climbing since 2006. As a result, the number of businesses in 2010 compared to 2007 is higher."

In 2013 Dun & Bradstreet estimates that there are more than twenty-three million small businesses in the United States, though between 2007 and 2012, the types of businesses have changed.

In 2007, there were six million small businesses in the "other services" sector, offering hospitality services and specialty goods, and 3.3 million small businesses in services like public relations and consulting. In 2010, those roles seemed to switch; recession customers cut other services and focused on buying business building-related services like outsourcing marketing and printing. In 2010, six million were providing "business services" while 3.3 million were providing "other services."

Small businesses represent 99.7 percent of all employer firms, employ about half of all private sector employees, and pay nearly 45 percent of the total U.S. private payroll.

Small businesses with fewer than five hundred employees export roughly $182 billion dollars a year or 29 percent of all exports.

I'll ask again: if you have or are thinking about starting a business, what's keeping you from success?

We asked this question on my radio show, and do you know what the number one answer was? It wasn't failure, as we thought. Most people who start a business believe in their ability to succeed but they are afraid to know what they don't know. Some small-business owners are afraid of new tools and technologies. They don't know what the new tools and technologies are, if they need them, how to use them, or what to pay the people who do. The funny thing is that some people *have* all the tools, technologies, or staff that understands them but then worry that people will know that they don't know how to use them. Sound familiar?

In essence, many business owners are held back from success by a lack of knowledge. They may think, "I have a great product, but what do I do next?"

The good news is that it's a little big world out there!

### *Why a little world?*

The Internet levels the playing field for all, thanks to the World Wide Web and online social communications. Before the web, you needed to be a celebrity or an athlete to have your face, voice, and story everywhere. Now you can just have a profile on Facebook. You can afford to share your voice, and it won't cost more than time. It's easy to work like a pro from home with your own e-media tools that help you *Choose Surthrival* on the Internet playing field.

### *Why a big world?*

According to the World Internet Usage and Population Statistics, as of February 2013, there were

7,017,846,922 people in the world with 360,985,492 of those people using the Internet, showing the rise from the 2006 global total of 1,018,057,389. That number grows daily thanks to efforts that cross the digital divide.

There has also been an increase of "Mom Internet users," many of whom use blogging to promote their home-based businesses.

What does the big world offer us? Opportunity! Fame! Money! Now is the best time to make money, become famous, and achieve success with a small business. What's keeping you from achieving it?

You need three simple components to have a successful business. Whatever your level of marketing, technology, social and e-media knowledge, or small-business knowledge, these steps make the difference between people who fail and those who surthrive with a home-based business.

## *The three success components*

The components are as follows:

1. Passion or belief: This translates into a product or service.

2. Strategy: A plan for marketing and selling your products.

3. Action: Implementing the strategy with actions that return sales.

Sound too simple? They are simple, but these components are proven by time. The most famous of the American outlaws used all components, and if you don't believe me, here is gun-slinging story that may convince you.

## *What Jesse James can teach today's business owners*

Jesse James is a famous outlaw who rode with his gang in the 1870s.

### Success Component 1: Passion

Jesse James had a passion all right; from boyhood, he was inspired by stories of Robin Hood. He believed that he could help people by robbing the rich and giving to the poor!

### Success Component 2: Strategy

Jesse James realized that his business of robbing from the rich to give to the poor would not work unless he created a plan. He asked questions like these: "How do I know who is rich and who is poor? What do we do after I rob them? How can we let people know what we are doing?" He knew that to rob banks and trains and get away with it, he would have to garner the compassion of the locals so that they would offer his band safe haven while they ran from the law. The strategy created from the questions led him to success, if you count robbing and shooting people as success, but for the sake of the example, let's continue.

### Success Component 3: Action

Once Jesse James had a strategy, he implemented it by taking action. The plan was to rob trains. The band identified the rich by their "plug hats" or "high hats" (tall cylindrical silk hats with a narrow brim) or by the look of their hands.

On the day of the first robbery, Jesse James sent what amounted to a press release to the local paper, declaring his intention to rob from the rich and give the money to Missouri farmers. The reporter had the story published in the paper before news of the train robbery leaked and gained popular support for James and his band.

You know the story. James robbed trains, shared the money with the farmers, and rode into legend by the power of the pen. He later named his son after the reporter who first told his story, and that reporter labeled the gang who eventually shot James in the back as cowards. Although the government celebrated, people in general mourned him as a sort of wild and misguided hero.

I'm sure that robbing trains isn't your chosen business, but my point is this: more than 140 years have passed since Jesse James employed the three success components to create a lucrative business, and we still know who he is. Consider implementing them before you start or continue your business.

## Question Six: Do You Have All Three Success Components?

If you have all three success components, there is nothing to be afraid of. Let's review the three success components checklist.

## Passion or belief: This translates into a product or service

What is your product or service? If you need help with that, read the next section or Question Seven, "Can you Color Your Own Parachute?"

## Strategy: A plan for marketing and selling your products

Having a strategy or a plan is essential so you don't throw away money on "spaghetti marketing" (throwing marketing out there to see what sticks!).

You can hire a consultant or marketing strategist, or you can learn to create a basic strategy yourself. You'll learn more about this in Question Eight, but in the meantime, helping business owners create and implement their strategies has been my life's work. You can learn how to create your own strategy in twenty-four hours by taking the course "24 Hours to Zero-Down Marketing," offered in the "Surthrival Series for Home-based Business Success." Step One helps you create a focused marketing strategy for your home business in twenty-four hours!

**Action: Implementing the strategy with actions that return sales.**

Once you have your strategy, it is time to implement it with tools that return sales.

If you need to face your fears about what you don't know about twenty-first-century tools and terms, I suggest steps two to five of the "Surthrival Series for Home-based Business Success" which gives you the information you need to make money on the Internet. We offer full e-media training and live and archived classes for your convenience. Learn what you need to know about marketing, selling, connecting, and competing online with the five e-media steps needed for home-based business success!

Twenty-first-century style means that you can do your own marketing, advertising, promotion, and selling online for less money and with less effort.

- Attract new business with social and e-media.

- Extend assistance to your customers online.

- Communicate 24/7 to potential clients.

- Introduce new procedures and solutions with e-media.

- Learn twenty-first-century tools to market your business for a lot less money and time!

If you can face the reality of what you need to succeed, and can check off (or plan to check off) the three success components, you may be a perfect candidate for a twenty-first-century home-based business!

# CHAPTER 7

# CAN YOU COLOR YOUR OWN PARACHUTE?

*Pick Your Favorite Passion!*

*"Find something you love to do, and you'll never have to work a day in your life."*

—*HARVEY MACKAY*

In the last chapter, we talked about the three success components. If you can check off all three success components on your own list, you could pass over the next few questions, or you may want to continue reading.

## *Passion = product*

Let's focus on the first component: passion or belief and the possibility of turning it into a product or service. You can turn almost any passion into a product or service with two disclaimers:

Your product or service must be legitimate.

Your product or service must have value.

What do I mean by legitimate? You can't start a small business and be successful if your product or service is a fake gadget, or gizmo. People don't like being swindled, and they will never give you a second chance if you do that. Success doesn't thrive in that type of situation, and neither will your business.

Your product or service must have value to someone and to society. For example, does a dog tongue scraper have value? Yes, to the people who are always kissing their dogs and want their pups to have good oral hygiene. It is a narrow consumer group, but the product does have value to them.

If you have a product that has value to anyone, anywhere, congratulations! You are ready to go on to the next step and create your marketing strategy.

### *"What color is your parachute?"*

When I was a little girl, I often heard people say, "What color is your parachute?" I never knew what that meant or that it was a highly respected career guide until my dad gave me a copy of the book and waved me off to university.

My dad, whose father had worked in a coal mine and in a factory, was excited that times had changed. Instead of following his father's footsteps, he came to California and was an entrepreneur, a real business man. No factories or mines for him, and he wanted the same opportunity for me.

*What Color Is Your Parachute?* was written by Richard Bolles, an Episcopal priest who was laid off during the 1960s, and he took an administrative position where he advised ministers of colleges around the country. When he found that these ministers were worried about what would happen to them if they lost their jobs, he wrote a guide to allay their fears. He gave away a few copies of his guide and received many more requests. The "viral marketing" resulted in sales of six million copies since he wrote the guide in 1968. His book is about recognizing what you excel at and finding a job that you love.

The book helped me decide what studies I should pursue, but I did not pick it up again until I graduated. After an internship in New York and studies in Japanese, I went to work for a company in Japan. While there, I realized a few things. I wasn't cut out to succeed in a male-dominated culture. I missed speaking English, and as shallow as this may sound, third, I was sick of eating sushi and sashimi and having to choose clothes that were way too short for me. I was unhappy.

After two years, I came home, moved back into my parents' house, and found myself wondering about my career. I picked up an old copy of *What Color is your Parachute?*, read it again, and decided to find a job that I liked.

In an interview with *Fast Company*, Richard Bolles said, "If you don't take time to figure out what you want to do with your life, you will be at the mercy of all those forces out there today."

He also said, "Today's jobs are essentially adventures. You never know what's going to happen next, and you must find job satisfaction in the work itself. Your self-esteem must come from doing the work rather than from some hoped-for promotion, pay raise, or other reward—which may never materialize."

For all of the changes since the days of the Nixon administration, the book's core advice hasn't changed. Finding a job is all about strategy. Choose the right strategy, and you can snare a good job even in bad times. Choose the wrong strategy, and even roads paved with gold will lead you nowhere.

For me, finding a job I would enjoy and excel at came, much to my father's chagrin after spending a fortune on my tuition, when I decided to work for Nordstrom. I started as a sales clerk, found I had a talent selling men's sportswear, and after a few years (spending most of my paycheck on clothes), I decided that I was good enough at sales to make more money elsewhere.

Following the book's advice, I started pestering people to give me an informational interview and met a woman who, after appraising my resume and seeing that I had a communications degree, Japanese experience, and sales experience, sent me to a friend who owned a PR firm in Newport Beach. This firm's clients were mainly Japanese, so it was a great fit. I worked there writing press releases for Suzuki, Yamaha, and Panasonic, selling their wares through words.

A friend I had known in Japan heard that I was working in PR and recommended me for a job: working as a press secretary for a man who was running for the U.S. Senate. He was last of four for his party's nomination, and was scrambling for funding. I accepted the challenge, although it meant leaving Newport Beach for Salt Lake City, Utah. I worked on a team with some great people including Richard Paul Evans, and we combined our skills to help Robert F. Bennett acquire his U.S. Senate seat. During the "Bennett for Senate" campaign, I created and used the strategy, "Make, Bake, Shake and Rake"—the same strategy I offer in my trainings for companies that want to succeed but are starting with a bootstrap budget. My strategy has never failed in the fifteen years since it was created, and it has been invaluable for businesses that want to go from survival to success.

Today, I think that the ideas in *What Color Is Your Parachute?* fit for small-business owners. As a society, we are no longer limited to finding a "job" where we work to support our families and make someone else rich. In 1988, my father, a self-made business success, never expected me to start my own business when he handed me that book. He just hoped that my college education would lead me to a job that I enjoyed. Today, there is much support for those who want to start a business doing what they enjoy. If you need work, write down the things you love. Then find a job doing those activities or start a business selling them.

## *How do I find something I love that makes money?*

My husband, Chad, asked me the same question. He was at a tough point in his life. After working for years as a police officer and going to school part-time, he graduated in aviation. However, he could not find a job in that industry that would support his family. He did what he was good at but had yet to excel at supporting his family financially. He tried working in my business, hated it, and was ready to throw out the book my father had suggested, *Do What You Love, The Money Will Follow.*

I had him get a piece of paper, sit in a peaceful spot, and write down what he loved doing. His list looked like this:

- Airplanes

- Guns

- Outdoors

- Adventure

- Health and Fitness

I said, "Okay, now write what you are good at doing." He wrote the following:

- Flying airplanes

- Shooting guns

- Hiking

- Defying death

- Working out

I said "Okay" while laughing at his attitude. He had worked hard at doing the things he loved and was worried that he would have to sit behind a desk for the rest of his life. I tried this: "What talents do you have?"

He said, "I don't know!" After being encouraged to be open and honest had, he said, "I'm a pretty good writer, I like to help people, I like to teach, I take tests well, and am good under pressure."

We looked at options for using those skills in the areas he loved, and we contacted people he knew and asked questions. Could he find a job teaching flying? Could he find job with police work or flying or outdoors? Could he find a job helping people with fitness?

He looked into all kinds of careers and business opportunities, and after a few weeks of research, soul-searching, and honest assessment,

He decided to volunteer as a first responder at our local fire department to keep himself in the throes of adventure. He didn't get paid, but the service was good for all involved.

Finally, through his volunteer work he found he could work as a police officer with the local County Sheriff who owned an aviation division. If he worked hard enough he could eventually fly for them.

Chad also found he could partner with my brother, Dennis, who had started a service that provides training and certification for people who want concealed weapon permits. The customers registered through a website to take live classes. The job, though part-time, paid $100 an hour—a helpful supplement to the hourly wages in law enforcement.

Chad acquired a job with the Sheriff's Office and is now doing what he loves full-time as a police officer, supplementing his income by teaching, and at the same time is working on a master's degree in holistic nutrition and fitness; where after he retires he will use his talents in an area that he also loves, and that will bring additional income to support the family. This way he might make enough money to support his family *and* realize his dream of flight. His skills at writing and testing serve him well in police work, pursuing additional education, and aviation.

The result? He is happy. Chad "colored the parachute" of his dreams in a way that fit his needs and the needs of his family and his passion. Failure turned into success by taking another look at doing what he loves!

## *Find a solution, wrap it up in a box, and pass it on*

Working in the radio business allows me to meet interesting people from all over the world who, while searching for a remedy for their own ills, have found solutions that turned into a business. For example, parents whose children face health issues often find solutions and then pioneer organizations to help their family and others. People are amazing in this way. When they find a good solution, they don't keep it to themselves—they pass it on.

We commonly hear about problems related to the increase in childhood diabetes, celiac disease, and other food-related issues. I was privileged to meet a man on my radio show who, when faced with a food-related issue in his family, went on a quest to find a solution.

Rod A. Smith, founder of The Green PolkaDot Box and the national "clean food" education movement, created a resource to those searching for affordable access to healthy food. While researching a solution to his own eating needs, he met industry leaders who challenged him to create national consumer access to organic foods that are not genetically modified (GMOs). He rose to the challenge and exceeded it by creating the nation's first online buying collective. It offers members lower pricing on healthy food and products directly from manufacturers and growers. The Green PolkaDot Box is an education portal for those seeking to learn about eating raw, organic, and natural foods and to understand food-related issues such as diabetes and gluten intolerance.

Smith created a solution that not only helps his own family but hundreds of thousands of others. The road to making affordable, organic, natural products available online was not easy. He overcame huge challenges and antagonism to make what's now called "The Box" a huge online success.

*My family gathered around our first order of organic foods from the Green PolkaDot Box. Learn how their referral rewards program helps families earn healthy food by visiting choosesurthrival.com or greenpolkadotbox.com/powermom.*

Rod Smith could have kept the savings on organic food solution to himself, but instead, he turned it into a resource for people who cannot otherwise afford clean food. I have heard many people say that because of The Green PolkaDot Box, they have been able to use their current budget to feed their children better food, keep them healthy, and decrease their healthcare costs. Healthier families and a healthier pocketbook seem like wonderful solutions to pass along.

Learn how The Green PolkaDot Box referral rewards program helps consumers earn healthy food by visiting my preparedhousewives.org or choosesurthrival.com.

## *Making a business out of giving back*

*"There's no limit to what a man (or women and their families) can achieve if he doesn't care who gets the credit."*

—*LAING BURNS, JR.*

*Kim Power Stilson with Holly Robinson Peete of the HollyRod Foundation at an Academy Awards Fundraising Event in Hollywood.*

Inspired by a father and a son, The HollyRod Foundation was founded by actress, author and philanthropist Holly Robinson Peete and her husband former NFL great Rodney Peete.

The foundation started when Holly's father was diagnosed with Parkinson's Disease and then when Holly's son was diagnosed with Autism it progressed to also include compassionate care for children with autism. The HollyRod Foundation is a great example of what people do to provide solutions and awareness for not only their families but others as well. Hollyrod.org.

Social enterprises are at the heart of many small businesses, and these businesses are finally getting the recognition they deserve in the form of funding from governments.

On the Financial Mail Women's Forum, which just won a prestigious award in 2013 for helping women reach the highest ranks possible in British business, Helen Loveless stated that the British government is behind an initiative that will create one hundred and fifty thousand jobs with companies that are set up principally on social enterprise.

Through talk radio show hosting, I have met thousands of men and women who have turned social enterprise efforts into business opportunities that help thousands more and make money. Could there be a better combination? It used to be that people felt embarrassed about asking for money unless it was for a cause. Even then, people asked, "How much of this donation goes to the cause, and how much goes into the pockets of those who run the organization?"

Now, thanks to all the online information, you can read information posted by industry watchdogs real-time instead of waiting for the media to expose corruption. Social enterprise—sharing to help others make money to support their causes and themselves—is more acceptable. It should be. We all need to take care of each other. If we don't support those who give their lives to passions that make the world a better place, how will it ever be a better place?

If you have a cause, turn it into a business, and do great things with the money you make! Success isn't just about money, but what if you could change the world and make money to send your kids to college too?

## Question Seven: Can You Color Your Own Parachute?

What is your passion? You may have that answer. If not, get a piece of paper, sit down in a peaceful spot, and answer these questions.

## How do I find something I love that makes money?

**What do you love?** Make a list.

*For example:*

Gardening

Fixing things

Teaching

Adventure

**What you are good at doing?**

*For example:*

Traveling

Golfing

Entertaining

**What talents do you have?**

*For example:*

I like to help people, I like to teach, and I am organized.

**Now compare and combine the lists.**

*For example:*

Could you find a job teaching golf? Yes.

Could you find a job entertaining people who travel? Yes.

Could you find a job organizing entertaining travel for people who like to golf? Yes.

### Do some research

Is there a need for any of the activities that you love to do? Is there a way to combine them and form a business? Are there businesses out there that do what you like? Can you fill a niche and start your own? Look into careers and business opportunities, and ask questions.

### Find people who are living a life you love, and copy them!

Some of the most successful people in the world advocate this advice. Find people you admire, and ask them what they do and how they learned to do it. Napoleon Hill tells a great story about this in his book *Think and Grow Rich*, and it could serve as a jumping board for your own small business!

There is a lot to be said for jumping on the bandwagon with a direct-selling business. Direct selling is the marketing and selling of products directly to consumers away from or independent of a retail location. Direct selling is daughter to door to door peddling which is the oldest form of direct sales. Unlike peddling, direct sales can not only be done door-to-door demonstrations but also through internet sales. Paul Zane Pilsner is a world renowned economist, bestselling author of several books and predicts that selling a product directly is the way to go for the future.

Together as a family, we started selling gourmet storable meals as part of a dinner table challenge to get families back to eating together at the table. GOFoods makes healthy, convenient meals that can be eaten anywhere from the dinner table to camp outs and can be stored with peace of mind that comes from knowing your family will always have delicious meals no matter what the future holds. We sell meals that not only provide an easy-to-fix dinner-time solution saving time for families but they also come in a mouth-watering variety from *Tuscan Sun Dried Tomato Pasta* and *Cheesy Chicken Cheddar* Rice to *Almond Granola*. These storable meals are sourced are sourced from American Non-GMO farmers and blended and packed fresh in a way that makes them storable for up to 25 years, unopened. We have a blast selling GOFoods Global's scrumptious products and they make it even more fun because they offer discounts to people in the Armed Forces. Plus for every 10 meal packages sold, one meal package is donated to local food banks by the GOFoods Foundation committed to feeding and prospering American families. As a family we enjoy learning about the food and emergency-preparedness industry and helping people eat a good healthy meal at their dinner table. Every time we sell a meal we make a little commission and every time we sell ten we are helping fund food banks. To get started we did not have to worry about creating a product, inventory, sales set up, or a website. We use e-media to market our message and product, and GOFoods does the rest! See what we are doing at dinnertable.mygofoods.com. You may want to look into direct-selling companies to see if one has a product that fits your passion.

Take the time to analyze your features, examine your passions, assess your skills and talents, and decide if you have the first component necessary to have or create a successful twenty-first-century home-based business!

# CHAPTER 8

# DO YOU HAVE A STRATEGY?
*Use Mine—It has Never Failed!*

*"What's the use of running if you are not on the right road?"*

—*German Proverb*

Once you have a product or service, you have your foundation for a business, and the next success component is strategy.

Several years ago, I was working for a software firm that was anxious to get its message out. We were short staffed and underfunded, but we still had a job to do. Sound familiar? I put together a marketing strategy on a bootstrap budget that covered all the angles of marketing without spending the fortune usually attached to such efforts.

Our plans were less extensive or generous, but they were concentrated and succeeded in taking our company from a 126 ranking in the industry to 3 (yes, the top three!) in nine months. We did it 60 percent under budget by using the Internet, World Wide Web and online social communications mixed with traditional marketing. My company could have paid a thousand times more for advertising and not received the success that we did with this plan. It was quick to recognize this and gave me a huge promotion and a raise. Obviously the plan worked. I made a few tweaks and adjustments to the plan, turned it into a duplicable strategy, and "Make Bake Shake & Rake" was born. Later I added another step, Fresh!

## *What's in a strategy?*

Make, Bake, Shake, Rake & Fresh® (MBSR&F) is a strategy that keeps you from throwing your money around without a return in sales. I have used the MBSR&F plan to successfully promote products, services, people, and companies, and it has never failed even with an adjustment of budget.

According to Harry Beckwith's book *Selling the Invisible,* some companies believe that sales and customer service are jobs for sales and customer service staff only. A CFO he knew lost his company a sale of $50,000 because he was neglected to use customer service skills and was rude to a customer.

> *"Everyone in your company is responsible for marketing your company. Every failure is likely to be costly."*
>
> —*HARRY BECKWITH*

What a company does with its marketing attention—sales force follow-through, customer service, product delivery, and commitment to process and duration—are the responsibility of every person in the company. Good company-wide marketing begins with commitment to a good marketing strategy, whether you have a team or you *are* the team.

You may not know exactly what to do, but decide today to do something, and stick to a cohesive, regularly applied marketing plan. Everyone who has used my process has succeeded in bringing attention and marketing focus to his or her company and its product or service.

Again, MBSR&F is a marketing process that has led to millions of queued sales, millions of dollars in funding, mention in the most prestigious media, and increased productivity at an average of 60 percent less than budgeted. All that from strategic marketing? Yes!

### *Will everyone buy donuts?*

MBSR&F is a recipe for success by marketing and positioning on a bootstrap budget. I have used it over and over with great success. To start, like any good recipe or approach in life, you Make an idea. You come up with the mission, the reason for proceeding, and the benefits of the goals you wish to accomplish.

For instance, I once worked with a man who had created a great software product that he wanted to release to the marketplace. It worked, it was a cost-effective solution, and it was ready to sell. The only problem was that he needed to tell people it was available. He needed a marketing strategy.

The first questions I asked were basic: "Why did you create this product?" and "Who are your customers?" He looked at me and said, "What do you mean? Everyone will buy it! It will be in every household!" I said, "Great. Who will buy it?" This intelligent man looked at me, not understanding, and said again, "Everyone!"

You would be surprised at the number of people who are not sure how to answer basic questions about their products and services. "Everyone" is a grand goal yet more likely to apply to selling donuts than software. "Everyone" would not be a good answer for donuts either. Some people are gluten intolerant, diabetic, watching their cholesterol, or live in a country where people have no any idea what a donut is and perhaps wouldn't like it if they tried it.)

*Who will buy your product? The answer is essential, but first you need to ask the right questions. Make, Bake, Shake, Rake & Fresh will help you determine what the right questions are.*

—KIM POWER STILSON

## Make & Bake

The Make part of the strategy helps you identify the ingredients of a product/service by contemplating what the mission is, what the message is, and how you can build a message for the product/service. You articulate the message in a form that everyone from the creators to future purchasers can easily understand.

Once the product is created and its message is clear, you still have to make sure it will Bake to its completion. Your team (you or you and a staff) must test the finished message for the product/service and ask these questions: "Does it work?" "Does it fit the niche we've placed it in?" "Does it have the value for which it was created, or does it fit somewhere else?" The baking process is essential; if you can find flaws before the "cake" falls, you can service the product, change the ingredients, and work out any flaws before you deliver the product and the consumer finds errors.

## Shake

The Shake stage happens once the product/service is ready to go! It is only then that a commitment is made to the world and the message is disbursed to the target markets. Shaking means sharing your message with everyone from potential customers to third-party validators (people who influence potential customers) in hopes that they will share their specific connection to the product with your target audience.

My grandfather liked to run rocks through a polisher as a hobby after a hard day at work. He used to say, "Leave no stone unturned" and found some gorgeous stones after running them through the polisher. That oft-used phrase is the rule here. During this stage of the process, share your message with everyone and in every way possible, which in the days of yore meant leaning over the fence to talk to a neighbor, posting flyers on telephone poles, or making phone calls like crazy.

Shake means to get your message out to every possible medium, both traditional and nontraditional, through its gatekeepers. This includes writers for traditional television, radio, and magazines to social media like blogs, wiki articles, downloadable video, and streaming radio shows. Continue until everyone in every category that relates to your product/service has been contacted. Many companies neglect this step despite its importance in achieving the desired results, but giving attention to this stage of the process has brought me great success.

I was once asked to market a produce that was ridiculously difficult to explain. It was a hardware/software combination that I had to introduce to the networking world. My target audience was technical resellers who didn't read national journals. My challenge was to apply MBSR&F and deliver a message to a narrow vertical market that I had never reached before.

For the Make stage, my team and I had to study the target customers or "techies" first hand. We found them to be abnormally intelligent and not easily distracted. We knew that they ate lunch at their desks (mostly fast food and frozen burritos) and spent more than twelve hours a day at their computer. We knew that they liked gadgets and only pulled focus from their computer screens when a new technology was introduced. Fluffy, cutesy magazine ads would not work, so we had to come up with a campaign appropriate for this audience.

As we implemented the Make and Bake stages, I was able to better understand the audience I was working with, thus enabling me to build a strategy. I named a rather ambiguous aspect of the product Fusion Port Technology and created a character named Fusion Port Dan, all based on the creator of the product and the topics that would interest our target techie.

For the Shake stage, I created a campaign that consisted of a series of postcards and follow-up packages showing the Fusion Port Dan character exploring the world of Fusion Port Technology. We sent the postcard and followed up with a touristy present from Fusion Port Dan on his travels.

On one postcard, I put a graphic of Fusion Port Dan sitting on a horse, looking out over one of the Egyptian pyramids through binoculars. A note on the postcard implied that Fusion Port Technology was durable and well-built enough to withstand the tests of time, much like the pyramids. We followed up one week later with a souvenir package containing a pair of binoculars and a fact sheet on the product.

Two weeks later, we began to receive calls from resellers who had received calls from our target techies, wanting to know about this new product. This all happened even before we mailed the second wave of the series. We received calls from resellers who were irritated at not having heard from us about our product before their customers, the techies, called them. Having learned something, we added the resellers to our Fusion Port mailing list.

Our lonely list of six resellers quickly increased to more than one hundred. We also received a call from an investor who wanted to discuss the future of our company and a partnership with his large technology company. He'd been informed of our new technology by one of the techies on our mailing list. Talk about shaking things up! Still, we didn't rest on our laurels. As soon as successful sales were in, it was time to Rake.

## Rake

Once a company has found success from the Shake stage, meaning any success at all, it needs to turn that into more success.

When we saw that our initial campaign strategies had worked, we turned that response into a cause to increase our success. We did this by sending press releases to the media and using magazines to reach more potential resellers. One magazine wrote about our "Award-Winning Fusion Port Technology," so we included that article with the mailers. When a new reseller or new partner signed up with our program, we sent out a press release explaining how and why they had joined our team. We made sure that everyone on our list received a copy of the release.

This strategy spread like an epidemic. Resellers who had ignored our initial mailers saw that other resellers had joined our team, and not wanting to miss out on the benefits of this new product, they called us to sign up.

One of our regional salesmen fought to get an appointment with a specific client. He heard that this client was going to entertain bids for a category that would fit our new product perfectly. He finally went in for his appointment, sat down in their office, and noticed our Fusion Port Dan postcard on the client's desk. The salesman said, "That's the product I am here to tell you about." The client said, "You're kidding! I love this campaign! I have been meaning to call you guys and had no idea you were from the same company!" That meeting resulted in an $8 million order and awestruck treatment from that salesperson who then called me (the "marketing person") his new best friend. I was his best friend because I was responsible for warming his sales lead into a hearty commission.

The Rake stage is important for one simple fact: focus leads to sales, but customers are busy people!

---

*It takes at least eighteen repetitions of hearing about a product before a person registers the information and decides to act.*

---

Marketing has to be delivered with this statistic in mind. Sending a message in mixed forms of media allows the count to reach eighteen faster. Receiving a message through various media allows people numerous chances to register it and decide what to do with the information. While the Shake portion of the strategy ensures that the message will be repeated everywhere, the Rake stage takes the message and delivers it home.

Let's say that your product is featured in your target magazine or in a blog, written by a third-party validator. You think, "Wow, we have made it!" and you wait for the clicks or the phone to start ringing— and you wait! Perhaps, the potential customers you targeted did not read the magazine or that blog that week. Maybe they did and landed on your website only to leave disinterested because your site content did not reflect your message and convert them to sales. Remember, people are busy, and you usually get one chance to make your sale.

The Rake stage ensures that they get another chance to register your message. You could Rake the message home by bookmarking the article, e-mailing it, or clipping the information and sending it directly to the consumer. One of my favorite ways to do this is by using Post-It® notes. I stick a Post-It note on the article, write "John, wanted to make sure you saw this!" on the note, slap it on the article, and mail it. To Rake, you don't have to use snail mail; you can blog, e-mail, micro blog, create a website landing page, bookmark, or get really creative and pick up a phone. I have received many thank-you notes and calls from busy people who appreciated my thoughtful communication. That thoughtful communication was part of the Rake stage and designed to share information about my product.

## *Fresh*

I added the term Fresh to my strategy with the advent of Web 3.0 and social interactive media. Fresh is an adjustment for the times. When I started my career, everyone was making money, and no one suspected that the dot-com bubble was about to burst. I used to e-mail when there was no one to e-mail. In fact, my boss would let us send e-mail, print the replies, and distribute them once a week in the office. Can you imagine that? Checking your e-mail once a week? If my boss had kept that up, by now we would have used up the world's forests!

Not long ago, you could devise a marketing strategy, print hundreds of brochures and collateral for a series of trade shows and sales events, and with a few campaign theme flyers tossed in, call it a year. Now, thanks to new technology, last quarter's brochure is already outdated, websites are updated frequently, e-blasts go out weekly, and blogs are written hourly. I didn't keep up with these activities before, but now I do, and so should you. Fresh, the crowning aspect of the strategy lets you keep your product/service fresh by doing all the steps you need to do without losing your mind. If waiting for my boss to hand me my e-mail reply was frustrating then, how about now when I get hundreds of e-mails every day?

I once counted how much time I spent answering e-mail in a week and saw a problem. It takes people ten seconds to dash off an e-mail; they believe that means they have communicated to you, and they expect a reply right away. While I hosted a radio show, I got several e-mails by the time my show finished— some irate that I hadn't answered yet! "I was on the radio until just now, and you were listening! Did you think you were listening to a clone?" I wanted to write back, but you can't do that. The best you can do is find ways to keep the marketing fresh. *24 Hours to Zero-Down Marketing* will give you strategies that keep your product/service communications fresh and keep you sane.

If you have a product that has value to anyone, anywhere, congratulations. You are set! Now you should, can, and will start creating your marketing strategy with Make, Bake, Shake, Rake & Fresh.

How do you get it? It is all there for you in Step One: Strategy! of the "Surthrival Series for Home-based Business Success."

*24 Hours to Zero-Down Marketing,* Step One, shows the fastest and most effective way to stay at home and make money with a strategy that works. It will give you a Make, Bake, Shake, Rake & Fresh strategy, directly focused on your own company, in twenty-four hours.

> *"The most intelligent man {person} living cannot succeed in accumulating money—nor in any other undertaking—without plans that are practicable and workable."*
>
> —*NAPOLEON HILL*

If you are ready to accuse me of shamelessly pitching my own wares in this guide, you are right, I am! I believe in my formula and the shattering story behind why I stopped everything to write training for the MBSR&F strategy, that has *never failed* when applied, is at the end of this guide. It works, and business owners who have used it say you can't afford *not* to have it! If you can you spare twenty-four hours to create a plan that will help your business succeed, you are on your way to sure surthrival!

## Question Eight: Do You Have a Strategy?

Do you have the second success component, strategy? Do you have or can you create a strategy to market your product or service? If you do, congratulations. You can check that off your list and move on to the next question.

If not, consider taking Step One: Strategy! of the "Surthrival Series for Home-based Business Success" which shows the fastest and most effective way to get a strategy that will work into your budget, busy schedule, and business. It's a step-by-step training that helps you create a marketing strategy, with all the necessary components from messaging to social and e-media, within twenty-four hours. You can get it at choosesurthrival.com. To inquire about scholarships and discounted tuition, kimpowerstilson@gmail.com.

You can do all the assignments in a twenty-four-hour spree, or you can break up the process for your convenience. Twenty-four hours may seem dramatic, but the sooner you laser-focus your time on efforts that result in sales, the better.

# CHAPTER 9

# ARE YOU READY TO MAKE DOUGH FROM HOME?

*Mompreneur Madness and Magnificent Bread makers*

*"The rising influence of women will be one of the most powerful transforming changes of this century."*

—MADELYN HOCHSTEIN , PRESIDENT DYG

One reason that the twenty-first century is the perfect time for home-based business success is because of the Internet. Having a working knowledge of social and e-media tools, terms, and practices allows you to converse with anyone around the globe from home. I can be on Skype with a colleague in Ireland, cooking dinner, texting my engineer, and posting a press release on Facebook and my business blog, all while monitoring my kids from home.

I'm doing what women do best—juggling—but doing it from home and more effectively thanks to the Internet. The practice is called social media, and it's as simple as people using the old-fashioned "grapevine" to connect for a purpose. Now that connection happens online.

*"Social media is the act of human society and organizations going online via the Internet and using its tools to focus on the needs, interests, and intentions of other people."*

—KIM POWER STILSON

The Action we talked about earlier (the third success component) is easier if you know how to use the tools well enough to implement your strategy. Social and e-media tools will be covered within this chapter as well as real-life, home-based business examples of moms who do it right. Before we talk about the tools, let's talk about the success the tools have achieved in a global perspective.

## *Can social media make a president?*

A historic election process set a precedent that changed the way America campaigns.

According to National Public Radio, it was a phenomenon. November 4, 2008! Election Day, and the two years that led up to it, were historically significant because for the first time, the Internet played a robust part in the election. They were talking about social media.

Like never before, the candidates used websites, web-posted press releases, online advertising, RSS feeds to news sites, blogs, communities, bookmarking sites, Internet TV and radio, search engine optimization tools, links and back links, Technorati links, Alexa ranking, page strength, indexed pages, and index rankings to determine their fate.

The social media applications in the campaign were mindboggling. The candidates were the product, and the voters were the customers. The winner used the same cost-effective tools that you have available for promoting your business. The result? Enough sales to win!

If you compare some of the online marketing practices between the candidates, you will get an idea of what I mean. Again, you can learn how to use them in Step Two: Tools! of the "Surthrival Series for Home-based Business Success" but for now, just take a look at the following. Remember, the higher the number, the better.

**Number of back links to candidate-related websites**

Obama    734,395

McCain    199,813

*\* January 2008 article by Michael Jensen, SoloSEO*


**Number of links on Technorati (a social networking site)**

Obama 22,662

McCain 6,172

*\* As of January 2008, article in SoloSEO*

In these cases, you can see the huge difference in online activity between the candidates. As said on NPR, it was a phenomenon, and political campaigns and business marketing have never been the same. (You just had to watch what happened during the 2012 Presidential campaign to see what I mean.) Just imagine what social and e-media could do for your home-based business success!

## Mompreneurs, media, and money

*"At the dawn of the twenty-first century, American women vocalized their power and began to exert it. In the last few years marketers have begun to recognize the power of the pocketbook—and to play to it. The women's movement in its broadest terms, which has transformed society, is at last transforming the marketing arena."*

*—BERNICE KANNER*

If you found the above interesting, you may be wondering how the social and e-media phenomenon can relate to you. Let's start by reviewing a global phenomenon that is growing closer to home: Mompreneurs.

*"Mompreneurs are creative mothers/caregivers whose goal is to stay at home with those they care for without sacrificing income. From stay-at-home moms who make extra money by reselling garage sale finds on eBay to women who care for their parents full time and also run a full-fledged company, Mompreneurs are becoming more and more common and essential to the U.S. economy."*

*—YAKTIVATE*

Mompreneurs mind the store, the kids, the spouse, the ageing parents, the home, and the pets, all at the same time. If there ever were a group destined for stay-at-home business success, it would be moms.

> *In a survey of small business owners, 51.6 percent of all businesses were operated primarily from someone's home.; 58.2% of those businesses started by women with less than $5,000 capital.*
>
> *There are 8.1 million women-owned small businesses in the U.S. with annual sales of $1.3 trillion and employing 7.7 million people.*
>
> —*SOURCE: THE DAILY TRANSCRIPT/SAN DIEGO SOURCE, SEPTEMBER 16, 2011.*

### What does the world think that women blog about?

People think women and mommy bloggers write primarily about children, pets and gossip, according to an informal survey by Prepared Housewives.

### What are moms really doing?

Monetizing their mouth and heart to feed their families! The practice communication and moms are using the social media grapevine to do it.

### What's it worth?

An average online sales Mompreneur makes $1,000 to $60,000 per month from home!

## Why does it work?

How else? The age old, tried and true, grapevine!

*85% of women trust the referrals of family and friends over corporate advertising!"*

—**HARRIS INTERACTIVE**

## The Keys to Success?

## Learn to use the technology

For many women without a technology background learning could mean facing their fears. In the June 2012 issue of "O Magazine" Oprah Winfrey writes about her visit to reconnect with author and spiritual guru Deepak Choprah in India. She talks about she was impressed with the brave widows who lined the streets to beg or do whatever they must to feed and care for their families.

I am sure many women who have faced their greatest fears to do what they must do for their family can relate. Learning to use online communication technologies while a bit overwhelming could possible change your life situation in way begging for rupees never could.

*"The benefits of technology and a good product with a passionate mom extend far beyond benefitting one family -- moms efforts improve the social and economic opportunities of entire families, businesses and communities...And eventually the world."*

—**PAMELA PASSMAN**

## Learn to use Infoedutainment®

Infoedutainment® is the term I came up for healthy online social and e-media communications. Posts, blogs, comments, shares, and messages need to be informational, educational, or entertaining, or don't bother.

We will review the tools, terms, and practices of social and e-media next. You can also read Step Two: Tools! of the "Surthrival Series for Home-based Business Success" for a more detailed training on many of the social media applications.

### *Prepared Housewives*

*"Combine moms with their passion to feed their hungry families with a direct selling company, and you have the leaders of the next trillion-dollar industry."*

—*PAUL ZANE PILSNER*

*Terri Hatcher (Desperate Housewives Star) with Kim Power Stilson and Diamond Donna Root (Prepared Housewives Founders)*

Before getting to the terms and tools of social and e-media, I'd like to share the stories of a few women who have made a home-based business model work for them. The Prepared Housewives mission is to "raise the socioeconomic status of a million homes by helping moms feed and fund their families from home."

The Prepared Housewives share resources that make it possible for families to be self-sufficient and entirely funded from home. They use social and e-media to share their solutions and help other mothers and families do the same. This group is the next evolution of a Mompreneur solution to help families meet their own needs by marketing their stay-at-home businesses. I am proud to say that I am a founding member of Prepared Housewives and invite you to read the stories of these women who have found a profitable personal niche in the home-based business arena that reaches beyond funding their home to assisting the world. Look on Facebook for Prepared Housewives.

## *Thriving in the new economy*

Diamond Donna Root is one of the nation's leading authorities on understanding and stimulating human maximum performance and potential. As an author, speaker, business consultant, executive coach, and personal-development guru, Donna has assisted executives, athletes, actors, and individuals to develop the critical mental and emotional skills needed to thrive in any business or personal relationship. Donna has been recognized by Cambridge Who's Who for excellence in leadership, vision, mentoring, and coaching. She has also produced several courses on peak performance and personal empowerment. Donna shares her message about achieving transformational growth in her "Thriving in the New Economy" training. For more information about Donna Root and the Purposely Rich! Talk Radio Show, visit gettingpastyou.com.

*Working mothers, Jane Lynch of the hit TV Show Glee with Kim Power Stilson and Diamond Donna Root at a fund-raising event.*

## Diamond Donna Root shares her personal story:

"As an entrepreneur and single mother of five kids, I have long been accustomed to supporting my family.

Feeding and funding my family was something I did as I traveled the globe presenting and speaking on personal empowerment and business development with Donald Trump, Les Brown, and Brian Tracey. Although I love teaching and speaking internationally, I had to sacrifice so much in being away from my family. As a mother and provider, I did not only what I could but simply what was required to keep my family thriving. Four years ago, I arrived home from speaking in Canada, and my fifteen-year-old son asked if he could talk with me. He needed me to be home when he needed help with his homework. He said that he wanted me to spend more time at home or he would move in with his father.

That was a pivotal day in our lives. Now that my youngest is eight, and life isn't so hectic. I realize how much time I missed with my kids. I understand the pressure that moms feel, because I have been on both sides of the fence. I have been a wife supporting a husband through a decade of school as well as a single mom providing for all aspects of my children's well-being. The job of a mom goes far beyond providing financial well-being—the emotional, spiritual, and physical well-being of our families is crucial.

We are witnessing an interesting time in history; the amazing advances in technology have impacted our lives for good in ways we have not even begun to appreciate. Technology is impacting our lives. Artificial intelligence has replaced entire industries at a rate that we have never seen before. Although failed government has played a significant role in the current economic environment, technology is having an impact there as well. Jobs are in jeopardy now more than ever thanks to technology. As more moms are forced to leave their homes to work, there will be an impact on the family. The Internet has given us moms an odd boon—the very automation that will put our husbands and friends out of work is the technology that can make moms profitable from the kitchen.

Kim, the author of *Choose Surthrival,* is one of the moms committed to using technology to benefit her family. She saw the beauty of starting an organization where moms could change the nation by feeding and funding their families from home. Kim and I got together, and the Prepared Housewives organization was born. Prepared Housewives is a sassy title for the powerful cause of moms helping moms and families thrive in the new economy. Our goal is to help moms feed and fund their families from the kitchen! Our mission is to change the socioeconomic status of a million homes, starting with food and then helping moms fund their family's basic needs in any economic environment.

In times of economic crisis, food becomes a powerful currency to keep families safe. We can help moms get their family food for free. We are changing one home at a time with my "Thriving in the New Economy" training and my "Getting Past You" program for those engaged in Prepared Housewives.

Our mission is to have moms help other moms become self-reliant. We start with preparation.

There is freedom and safety in knowing that you have the basics covered, and it is in feeling free and safe that we thrive. Our first goal is to make sure that every family has food that is healthy, affordable easy-to-prepare and delicious. We contacted GOFoods Global, owned by Brad Stewart which provide healthy, gourmet, storable meals and pays families for sharing their message and products. This is only the beginning, and once we have our families fed, we can accomplish more with other companies and other products.

May starting your own home-based business help you find the peace of mind you've been looking for.

*GOFoods founders liked the idea of the Prepared Housewives so well they asked Kim Power Stilson (pictured above) and*

*Donna Root to speak about how families can help other families at their annual convention!*

## A healer in every home

Laura Jacobs has been a practitioner in the health and wellness industry for fifteen years and served over fourteen thousand clients. She and her husband, Jerry, have operated their Herbs for Health store for the last fourteen years in Pleasant Grove, Utah.

Laura is an herbalist and aroma therapist who practices iridology, kinesiology, nutrition, and life coaching, and she created her own health scan program that accesses holistic health using the latest technology. She searched for over a decade for an essential oil company and partnered with its direct sales program in August 2008 to build a stay-at-home business for her family and others. She has found immense satisfaction and success in her relationship with the company and its products. It allowed her to expand her sphere of influence to make a global impact and fulfill her mission of "a healer in every home."

As a Prepared Housewives cofounder, Laura uses e-media to share the healing power of essential oils and her "Healer in Every Home" education services, and she makes five times the amount of money she made in her retail store. She now has the time and resources to focus on her family while working from home and traveling the world. Laura focuses on teaching and training in an effort to support all those who desire a healthy, preventive lifestyle. To find out more join Prepared Housewives on Facebook.

## *Home fires*

Another Prepared Housewives supporter is Teresa Horvet. Her goal is to help moms feed and fund their families from home by helping people earn free energy credits to fuel their home. It's a powerful story.

"I have been a stay-at-home mom since we adopted our first child, our son, in 1999. Things were going along nicely. My husband had a steady job, and we were planning our second adoption—this time, going to China to adopt our daughter. During that time, my mother passed away. She left my sister and me a small inheritance.

My mother worked at the post office for thirty-five years. It began as a temporary job while my father was laid off from his job. Then my father became terminally ill and passed away when I was eight And then my mom worked nights and sleep during the day while my sister and I were at school. She encouraged me to find extra ways to bring in income, because relying on one form of income was risky.

While we had our paperwork finished and sent to China for approval, my husband was laid off along with his entire department. We went to China on a wing and a prayer that when we returned with our daughter, he could find employment. After six months of unemployment, I watched our savings and the inheritance dwindle. I then understood what my mother was trying to tell me. I knew that I had to find something that brought in extra money should this ever happen again.

I still wanted to be home for my children, so I thought about the criteria for a business that would fit my core values. I did not want a business that took me out of my house. I wanted a business that did not fill my home with products to sell to customers, and I did not have to take care of billing and shipping. I especially did not want a business that required my friends and family to buy my products for more than they would spend at the local store. Nothing fit my criteria.

One summer, everything changed. I overheard a woman talking to her friend about how much fun she was having in her company. I asked her who she worked for, and she gave me her card and told me about how her company helps people save on energy costs. That got my attention! A business that saves people money on something they have to buy anyway? I knew I had to investigate this further. I was pretty sure that I had finally found something that fit all of my criteria and my core beliefs. I was always telling people about current sales, arranging hand-me-down clothing connections, and referring people to businesses that offered great service at a fair price. In other words, I loved saving people money on the things they needed.

I am now able to stay home and be available for my children, and I love helping families create ways to expand their monthly budget and never worry about their energy bill again." Find Prepared Housewives on Facebook.

## Social and e-media: Let's get started!

*"There are some things you don't have to know how it works. The main thing is that it works. While some people are studying the roots, others are picking the fruit. It just depends which end of this you want to get in on."*

—*Jim Rohn*

For home-based business success in the twenty-first century, you need to be competitive and use the tools everyone else is using to get the sales that everyone else is getting.

Marketing a business is less expensive now than at any other time. With a little knowledge and time, any small-business owner can learn the basics of marketing.

In Question Eight, you learned how to develop a basic plan for marketing and selling your business. When you answer Question Nine, you will learn what you need to know and how to proceed. The freedom that comes from acknowledging that you don't know, and then learning how to do what you don't know, is immeasurable and inexpensive!

To start, the least expensive tool to start reaching your customers is found on the Internet using social communication.

## *The practices, terms, and tools*

Again, there are over twenty-three million small businesses in the United States, and only 5 percent are using social media, but the numbers are growing rapidly. In 2013, eMarketer predicts that the social networking population will reach 21.9 million. If you want to take advantage of the opportunities for your business, get going!

## *Practices*

Internet marketing practices include the following:

SEO or Search engine marketing

Web banner ads

E-mail marketing

Affiliate marketing

Revenue sharing

Internet TV and radio, audio, or video

Blog marketing

Viral marketing

Online identity management

## Terms

Do you know what the following terms mean?

Griefer

GUI

Klog

Blogosphere

Shoulder Surfer

Netiquette

All of the above terms are defined in the Appendix Terms section at the end of this book. Definitions were excerpted from Volume 12 of the "Surthrival Series", *Surthrival Terms*.

## Tools

Some basic tools you may want to learn if you have or are thinking about starting your own business are listed below. You need to learn whether they apply to your business.

avatar

Bing

blast

blog

bookmark

Facebook

Google

Hulu

link

ping

Pinterest

pod

release

RSS

Skype

smartphone

stream

tag

Twitter

video

web

widget

wiki

You Tube

Learning the tools to promote your business is imperative and the first part of the third success component, Action. Step Two: Tools of the "Surthrival Series for Home-based Business Success" training includes these courses:

- What are social and e-media, and how will they help my business?

- Learn how to use blogs, pings, pods, streams, bookmarks, blasts, releases, wikis, widgets, the web, links, avatars, tags, RSS, Twitter, Google, Bing, video, smartphones, Facebook, Skype, Pinterest, Hulu, and YouTube!

Before you check Action off your list, go to Question Nine to find out how to learn how to use and apply these practices, terms, and tools to your home-based business, and then come back to learn more about twenty-first-century sales.

## Question Nine: Are You Ready to Make Dough from Home?

Do you have the third success component, Action? Action requires knowledge of twenty-first-century tools, combined with sales, for success.

You may already be an online social communications whiz kid! Even if you have limited time, you can easily learn to use the practices, tools, and terms of social and e-media.

If you are ready to learn to use these tools efficiently and with flavor, you are ready to make dough from home!

# CHAPTER 10

# CAN YOU SELL?
## *Focus, People, Swoosh!*

*"Success isn't a result of spontaneous combustion. You must set yourself on fire."*

—ARNOLD H. GLASGOW

The person with the most sales volume wins!

According to Tom Egan, my partner in World Campus World Wide (WcWW) and cohost of the talk radio show E-media for Your Business, the essence of business sales success comes in threes. Here are Tom's thoughts on the essence of sales success.

1. **Focus! Focus with flame-like intensity.** Work each day as if your life depended on what you are doing.

2. **People! Make it your business to know them well.** Obtain a "master's degree in people," as people will make or break you. Learn what motivates them and causes them to do what they do.

3. **Swoosh! Just do it!** Like the Nike logo that stands for the slogan "just do it," Swoosh

means making those sales. As you just do it, you will make mistakes and correct them along the way. Most people talk about what they are going to do and never do it. Go for the Swoosh! The difference between success and failure is being the one who does it.

Three of the world's greatest salespeople, Napoleon Hill, Dale Carnegie, and Benjamin Franklin, agree with Tom. If you are not familiar with what they taught, here is a brief overview.

## *Napoleon Hill*

My father read *Think and Grow Rich* by Napoleon Hill at the suggestion of a friend in 1964. An immigrant from the UK who believed America to be the land of opportunity, my father left a lucrative electronics job to get into real estate. He went without pay for six months before achieving success, and he went on to start a nationally successful electronics company.

I pulled this book off my father's bookshelf years ago when I was starting as an entrepreneur. I found it to be odd and surely outdated, but there was a kind of magic in it that held me riveted to the end. It made me believe again that anything was possible.

*Think and Grow Rich* was inspired by a suggestion that Andrew Carnegie gave Napoleon Hill, and it was published near the end of the Great Depression, a time when the world needed that kind of magic to rebuild itself. I have friends from all over the world who read this book at some point in their lives. Perhaps that is why it has sold twenty million copies and why many websites share the magic of Hill's words. Ross Cornwell republished *Think and Grow Rich* in 2004 with a second printing in 2007, thirty-seven years after Hill died.

Hill shared in his writings that people are free to believe what they want and that this is what sets the United States apart from all other countries. Hill's works examined the power of personal beliefs and the role they play in personal success. One of Hill's hallmark expressions is "What the mind of man can conceive and believe, it can achieve."

According to Hill, 98 percent of people have no firm beliefs, putting true success out of reach, but sales of his numerous books prove that modern Americans still seek the secret of achievement. Hill's writings dealt with controversial subjects such as racism, slavery, oppression, failure, revolution, war, and poverty. I believe *Think and Grow Rich* should be required reading for today's entrepreneurs. You may need a dictionary for references like *mimeograph,* but the ideas in the book remain illuminating for anyone with an entrepreneurial spirit.

## Dale Carnegie

Another great book (to remind you of Focus, People, and Swoosh) is *How to Win Friends and Influence People* by Dale Carnegie.

I read it after the dot-com burst and the attacks of September 11, 2001, and a recent layoff had me looking for a job. As I read the first few chapters, laughing at the old-fashioned terms, I applied the principles and got a job before I finished it. The second time I read it, I found myself abandoned by business partners and left without dreams. I read the book from cover to cover, thought about a great idea that I had been too chicken to try, and succeeded a thousand times better than I had dreamed.

It is amazing that a book written in 1936 would offer suggestions that are both needed and applicable today, provided that you can get past references to Dictaphones, women's career limitations, and other old-fashioned sentiments. Although times have changed, the book covers basic ideas that human beings still need direction with: handling people, being liked, succeeding, and being a good leader. The advice is timeless, and the reading is both informational and historical.

Each chapter includes a summary, and Carnegie invites you to read each chapter twice. Carnegie was smart; he knew that reading it twice would increase retention and allow readers to become more successful. I read the chapters twice, and putting in twice the effort resulted in five times more success. Doubling your efforts can be a good investment! Test it yourself.

I had forgotten, amidst my woes, the simple things, and as trite as this may read, I loved his advice on holding your head high and the value of a smile. I thought of the number of customer interactions I had received and given without a smile, and made this small gesture—the best I could do at the time—with amazing returns. Carnegie gives both professional and spiritual reasons to smile, and as simple as it sounds, the world would truly be a happier place if we applied this one idea.

The book is full of powerful advice to help you become a more successful business owner, salesperson and human being. Carnegie's life and his book offer a creed worthy of striving for. If you have never read *How to Win Friends and Influence People*, make doing so a priority. Books written in that time period may sound dated, but the information is applicable for those who want to be successful.

You can find the book in bookstores and online. If you check, you might find it on your father's or a friend's bookshelf.

## *Benjamin Franklin*

*"Hide not your talents, they for use were made. What's a sun-dial in the shade?"*

—BENJAMIN FRANKLIN

In *How I Raised Myself from Failure to Success in Sales,* Frank Bettinger shares that he was born during a blizzard in 1888, and as a boy, he watched a man light the street lights with a blazing torch, leaving an illuminated path behind him. Later in life, recovering from career failure and looking for inspiration, he equated that experience to reading *The Autobiography of Ben Franklin.* Bettinger says, "Ben Franklin left a trail of lights behind him so that others could see their way."

Benjamin Franklin was not only one of the founding fathers of the United States; he was a writer, publisher, inventor, diplomat, scientist, and philosopher. He is well known for his experiments with electricity and lightning and for publishing *Poor Richard's Almanac.* He served as postmaster general under the Continental Congress and later became a prominent abolitionist. He is credited with inventing the lightning rod, the Franklin stove, and bifocals.

Ben Franklin chose thirteen subjects that he felt were necessary to focus on to become more successful. He gave each subject strict attention for a week, focusing on perfecting that subject with action and attention and carrying an index card with the subject information in his vest pocket. The next week, he moved on to the next subject and put the next index card in his pocket. He did this for thirteen weeks in a row and repeated the series four times in one year. It is said that with all his successes, Franklin claimed this as one of his best practices for success. Frank Bettinger said, "Reject this (plan), and you reject one of the most practical ideas ever offered you. I know what it did for me, and I know it can do the same for anyone who will try it. It's not an easy way. There is no easy way, but it is a sure way."

Why thirteen specific subjects? Perhaps to Franklin it seemed like a way to turn an unlucky number into a successful number of traits! Bettinger said that if a man with little formal schooling like Franklin could be showered with the highest honors for his successes, there must be something powerful in his ideas.

For me, the idea of focusing on one action each week to increase my success was less overwhelming than jumping into the list all at once. I was excited to make this practice part of my life and my business to achieve a better self. Surely with that kind of effort and one week of focus at a time, I would be more successful. I recommend this plan for anyone who is overwhelmed but wants to try the advice of one of the world's most successful individuals.

If you want a successful small business, you need to know how to make sales, lots of them! It's simple if you remember Focus, People, and Swoosh.

## Question Ten: Can You Sell?

Before you pursue a home-based business, you need to know how to sell and sell well. My brothers, Geoff, Dennis and Charles, can "sell ice to Eskimos." How did he learn to sell? He followed the sales essentials you just learned about from some of history's master salesmen.

With a twenty-first-century business, your sales plan will most likely not include selling door to door, but it will probably include selling website to website!

Selling is an art form, and there are many amazing books that you can read to learn how to succeed. I suggest Step Three: Sales! of the "Surthrival Series for Home-based Business Success." You can find this training at choosesurthrival.com or powerstrategies. TV. It is an inexpensive way to keep your finger on the pulse of your sales, past and present, especially if you have a busy schedule.

You could also read some of the fabulous sales books and courses available online and at your local library.

Congratulations on learning to use twenty-first-century e-media tools. Now you can check success component three, Action, off your list.

# CHAPTER 11

# READY TO ACHIEVE SUCCESS IN THE TWENTY-FIRST CENTURY?

## *My Glass-Shattering Story*

*"Success seems to be connected with action. Successful people keep moving. They make mistakes, but they don't quit."*

—CONRAD HILTON

Now that you have answered the ten questions in this book, you should know if you are ready to work at home for twenty-first-century success. I had to go on my own journey to find the answers to the questions.

### I had no idea I might die that day

In 2006 I spent ten days of the beautiful Manhattan autumn holed up in a hotel room, shouting at my assistants to get work done for the press tour for seven of our clients. I had worked hard. I had made a lot of money incorporating my Make, Bake, Shake, Rake & Fresh strategy into the marketing plans of business owners who were desperate to succeed. I helped thousands of small businesses share their messages online. My strategy had never failed to bring clients who adhered to it great success, yet I missed being home with my kids and sleeping in my own bed.

Have you ever worked so hard to make "enough money" that you don't have time to even think about spending it? I was there.

With my client's business successfully accomplished, I was the last to head home and had six hours before I had to catch my flight out of John F. Kennedy International Airport. There is a unique sensation to autumn in Manhattan; the trees were turning, the sun was out, and the air was crisp and clear. I was determined to enjoy it.

### What happens when you finally decide to relax?

I left my hotel on Fifty-Ninth and walked down Sixth Avenue toward Bryant Park. As I stepped into the crosswalk with the other pedestrians, I heard a resounding crack. I looked up to see what looked like a city-block-sized piece of cardboard wafting down over me. As I looked up, wondering what was above, a voice—the Holy Ghost, my guardian angel, the voice in my head, whatever you want to call it— shouted "Run! Shout run!" I knew I was in danger.

I shouted "RUN" to my fellow pedestrians and took off toward oncoming traffic. As I ran, I heard a big crash. Glass shards, nails, and bits of wood flew past me. In my suit and high heels, I ran like I had never run before…for my life!

All I could think was, "This is how it ends? I work hard to make $30,000 in one week, and I do not get to enjoy it, and I never get to see my family again?" I was showered with debris, but it didn't register as I kept running. Everything was in slow motion; I could hear nothing but my feet on the pavement and the beat of my heart. It was just like what you see in the movies, only this was real!

As the glass shattered, I prayed a promise. I vowed that if I lived through this, I would change my life. Instead of working hard to make more money, I would spend more time with my kids, treat people better, live a better life, and leave a legacy. How many times had I turned clients away because they could not pay my fees? If I died now, what would be left of me? No further income for my family?

I knew exactly what to do: write down everything I knew from my seventeen years of marketing success and share it with small-business owners at a price they could afford. I would teach them to do what I do so that they could do it themselves. Duplicating myself and sharing my talents would allow me to spend more time with my family, enjoying my success. We would all win! I had always felt prompted to do this, but why hadn't I listened? Was it too late?

I prayed as I ran. I promised that if I was saved, I would share my talents, I would give back. I prayed as I never had prayed before. I prayed to God, the God I now know is very real. As glass and boards screeched past me, I prayed my promise of living a better life if I were given another chance.

Suddenly, a hand pulled me under a concrete garage. Under the garage, I saw two pedestrians that I recognized from the crosswalk: a guy with a backpack and a girl in a Fifth Avenue suit that I had admired while walking behind her. Now her suit was covered in dust, and her stockings were blood stained and torn. The guy with the backpack pointed and said, "Look that is where we were standing! If you hadn't yelled, we would have been there! You saved us!"

In the crosswalk, I saw a pile of debris at least a story high. There was a cab in the crosswalk; it had come up over the curb when glass fell into the passenger seat of his car.

Under the shelter of the garage, we watched people running and shouting about September 11. The world seemed to come out of slow motion, sirens started wailing, and construction workers streamed out of a building, yelling, "Is everyone all right?" The glass had settled, but we were hesitant to come out of our shelter. When we did, we watched as the sobbing cab driver told his story to someone who was helping him out of his cab. "It came out of nowhere...I jumped the curb. I could have hit someone. The glass could have crushed me!"

I said to a construction worker, "I saw it falling and thought it was cardboard!" The backpack guy said, "We heard a crack, looked up, and if she hadn't shouted run, we would have been crushed!"

The construction worker said that the crew was lifting a large piece of glass by crane sixty stories up, something snapped, and the glass came crashing down. The large glass side of the building slipped down over the crosswalk, slammed into the building, and shattered, a piece coming corner-down into the cab driver's front seat. Glass, wood, and nails flew across four city blocks.

People began to come out from under cars and out of buildings, some torn and bloody but as far as the construction worker could find, none were seriously wounded. We were told to wait for the police, but as I heard sirens and saw people cautiously peeking out of buildings, I knew I could not just stand there.

I drifted from the group of pedestrians and walked into the nearest deli where people were asking, "What happened?" The guy at the counter gave me free soup after I told him I had been there. He said that I was lucky to be alive as he watched me brush bits of glass out of my hair. People swarmed around, and another person from the crosswalk joined me in answering questions. We repeated what happened, and the New Yorkers were friendlier in this crisis than I had ever seen them. It was like the city I visited months after September 11. Everyone was friendly, everyone cared, everyone was curious.

Still dazed, I walked a few blocks to Grand Central Station and sat there for hours. I was shaking, and I am sure I was in shock. I had to walk a long way back to my hotel; everything was cordoned off for blocks, but even so, I had no desire to venture near that area. When I got to the hotel and asked for my airport shuttle, I talked with the doorman about what happened. He said he had worked at the same place during September 11, and when he heard the sirens and saw the glass shards, the dust, and people running, even from two blocks away, he flashed back to the day. That day, he had started running himself and did not stop until he arrived home. He watched over me until I left, and refusing a tip, put me into the best limo he could find.

After I had flown home, I knew I was lucky to be alive as I watched the news reports with my family. For months, I jumped at any loud cracking sound, but I did not forget my promise. It has been more than five years since the glass fell, and indeed, I have changed my life.

**With a life-saving promise, isn't there always a catch?**

After that, I developed my marketing and sales strategies into a training series that gave business owners the opportunity to take charge of their marketing and sales without the help of an expensive consultant, as I promised.

When I asked to be spared so that I could change my life, I had no idea how difficult that would be. On one hand, writing about my MBSR&F strategy flowed effortlessly, and my experience became an easy-to-follow training series. On the other hand, life as I knew it fell apart. Clients that used to pay the big bucks disappeared with unpaid invoices. Businesses that I owned with partners, who expected me to put the usual time in, fell apart. It took every ounce of strength I had to keep writing and not go back to the previous client model to make money. I had made a promise, and I intended to keep it.

After eighteen months, I was out of resources, but my legacy was complete. My life was completely different. I was independent of any business ties but responsible only to my solely owned Power Strategies company and free to do anything I wanted with my life. I should have been scared, but I was oddly exhilarated.

I realized that I had become one of the companies I was trying to help! I had a company with a product that I needed to sell but didn't have the money to market. As my strategy was ready to share with the world, I decided to apply my own strategy to my own company. It was more than ironic that my promise to save my own life would save my business life—what a humbling realization that was!

I needed to apply the three success components. First, I got a strategy. I tested the training out on a few people who had asked for my advice and could not afford the answers. The people I shared it with loved it. One did so well that she turned her quilting material company, which had only been a hobby, into a full-scale online store. The strategy worked so well that her husband quit his full-time job to help her.

The next business owner's response was, "I was so busy running my business that I did not take the time to promote it; I did not want to tackle that task or learn something new. I threw away a lot of money and did not understand why I wasn't succeeding at marketing my product. Once I took the training, and I knew what to do. I added it to my list ,and the results were fantastic! It was so easy that I wish I would have done it years ago."

The second step was action. I applied my own strategy to market my company with twenty-first-century tools and sales. I had a shoestring budget, and with every sale, I put a few more dollars into marketing. I created my own strategy, did my own action, built my own website, and marketed my company.

## The Result

I saw the kind of success that every business owner desires: sales! While learning to make my website a success, I met and then partnered with Tom "Net" Egan. His group suggested that WcWW embrace the large numbers of people wanting to learn about e-media training for their companies. I won a "Social Media Marketer of the Year" award from an e-learning company. The legacy I am leaving is one that will help business owners market, sell, and compete online. You can read the "Surthrival Series for Home-based Business Success" at powerstrategies.TV or choosesurthrival.com.

## Have I kept my promise?

Yes! I went back to Manhattan this last autumn and walked the same path I had years before. On 6th Avenue there was no falling glass, just bits of autumn blue sky framed by scrapers, and business as usual going on around me. New York was oblivious to the change wrought in me since I had run for my life on that very street years earlier. Yet I had not and will not forget the chance I have been given to live and to change. I have also learned that going from surviving to thriving isn't always a home-based business motivation. In spring 2012, I was diagnosed with Hashimoto's Disease and while in New York I realized that everything I have learned from surviving the crashing glass onward has enabled me to deal well with this change in my physical health. Now my family and I also help other moms suffering from thyroid disease like me, by using e-media to promote awareness on <u>mymomisnothashimoto.com.</u> You never know what life will throw at you but choosing to thrive with passion, humor and style is always possible when you make a personal commitment and have the courage to keep it.

The "Surthrival Series for Home-based Business Success" gives stay-at-home business owners or hopeful owners the opportunity to start marketing their products on a bootstrap budget within twenty-four hours! It's an education in Internet and online social and e-media communications for home-based business families like me.

It is my hope that my advice, born out of a prayerful promise for your business, will let you lead the life you want to live. What you do with the success you achieve from following the "Surthrival Series for Home-based Business Success" is up to you, but I want you to have it. You don't have to make a promise during a traumatic, "glass-shattering" event like I did, but I hope that you enjoy your success and share it with those you love!

## Question Eleven: Can You Achieve Success in the Twenty-First Century?

I am living the life I wished I had been living while running from crashing glass. I am living it twenty-first-century style with e-media, and I am pleased to share my experience if it will help others live the life of success that they want. So, now it is your turn. Once again, answer these eleven questions:

Looking for Diamonds?

What do you want?

Is this the right time?

Will you put your oxygen mask first?

Do you know the secret to surthrival?

Do you have all three success components?

Can you color your own parachute?

Do you have a strategy?

Are you ready to make dough from home?

Can you sell?

Ready to achieve success in the 21st Century?

If you answered the questions, feel joyful and excited about life, and can't wait to pursue your business dreams, you have your answer. Your last assignment is to *Choose Surthrival* by creating a successful home- business!

Learn all you need to know about the basics of succeeding with your own business in the twenty-first century, adhere to the three success components, keep your mind open to learning more about e-media, and enjoy your own home-based business success!

CONCLUSION

# DUPLICATE YOURSELF
## *Grow Faster, Greener, and Easier with E-media*

*"When one door closes another door opens; but we so often look so long and so regretfully upon the closed door, that we do not see the ones which open for us."*

—Alexander Graham Bell

Questions asked, answers given, decisions made! If you have answered the eleven questions and feel like you are ready to promote your home-based business to garner the world's greatest reward— having a profitable business and being your own boss while staying at home with your family—you will not just survive you will thrive! Are you ready to power your dreams, power your life and power your dream with e-media?

You really can grow faster, greener, and easier with e-media. As a business owner, I can be online, training large groups of people from my e-media hub, while selling my services from my site and pacing the front entry waiting for my teenagers to come home! I can save paper, electricity, and my health, because

I am multitasking with less drain on my favorite resources. E-media makes your life simpler and more exciting and reaches beyond previously imaginable boundaries. I can tell you from my family business experience that it doesn't get any better than that! So what is getting in the way of your success but you?

> *"I've missed more than nine thousand shots in my career. I've lost almost three hundred games. Twenty-six times, I've been trusted to take the game winning shot and missed. I've failed over and over and over again in my life, and that is why I succeed."*
>
> —*Michael Jordan*

Many of us have suffered with the emotions and hardships that come from being unemployed, out of work, and undervalued. For all of you who have worked hard from your kitchen table, garage, or home office and kept trying, I salute you. You are not alone, and I hope to see your e-media messages online soon. Give it a try!

> *"The most practical, beautiful, workable philosophy in the world won't work if you won't."*
>
> —*Zig Ziglar*

I want you to have every chance to succeed, and I hope that this book helped you in your quest to *Choose Surthrival* with your own home-based business success!

# CONNECT WITH THE AUTHOR

*Kim Power Stilson hosting the TalkWorthy Radio Show on SiriusXM Channel 143.*

Kim Power Stilson has been described as a power and fame megaphone for business owners. Over the last seventeen years, she has helped hundreds of people make sure their messages were heard through fame and power positioning using tools like e-media, public relations, radio, and TV. Her clients range from Hollywood celebrities, United States Senators, and best-selling authors, to corporations, home-based businesses and family-owned non-profit organizations.

*Kim Power Stilson with daughter and friends at Birthday Bash for the American Cancer Society in Hollywood.*

As an award-winning talk show host and Pioneer of Internet talk radio, Kim has shared hundreds of people's stories live from the studio and remotely from events around the world, ranging from Bluegrass festivals in Ireland to fundraisers in Hollywood. You can listen to the *TalkWorthy Radio Show* live weekdays on SiriusXM Channel 143 and byuradio.org. To apply to be interviewed on the show, please visit talkworthyradio.com. To find out more about the talk shows Kim hosts please visit talkworthyradio.com

*Kim Power Stilson with Sugar Ray Leonard and his daughter at a fundraiser for juvenile diabetes.*

As the owner of Power Strategies, Inc. and an e-media strategist, Kim is a sought-after speaker for corporations, organizations, universities, and national publications. She is the author of several entrepreneur training products including 24 Hours to Zero-Down Marketing and the "Surthrival Series for Home-based Business Success" training series, which teaches people how to promote their business with e-media tools. Please visit choosesurthrival.com

A graduate of Brigham Young University, Kim speaks conversational Japanese, is the founder of the Bluebird Sisterhood, serves as director on several boards, dabbles at watercolor, plays tennis, snow skis, writes, and loves being near the sea. A dual citizen, she divides her time between the United

States, England, and Ireland. She has 3 children, an assortment of their rescued dogs and cats, and 1 very patient hero husband.

*Kim and assorted family and friends at a graduation event.*

Please connect with Kim Power Stilson on Facebook, Pinterest, GooglePlus, Twitter, LinkedIn and kimpowerstilson.com and email her at kimpowerstilson@gmail.com.

# APPENDIX

# BIBLIOGRAPHY

Beckwith, Harry. <u>Selling the Invisible.</u> New York, NY: Warner Books, 1997.

Bettger, Frank. <u>How I Raised Myself from Failure to Success in Selling.</u> New York, NY: Cornerstone Library, 1949.

Byrne, Rhonda. <u>The Secret.</u> Hillsboro, OR: Beyond Words Publishing with Atria Books, 2006.

Dossey, Larry. <u>The Extraordinary Healing Power of Ordinary Things. Boston, MA: Dutton, 2009.</u>

Ferriss, Timothy. <u>The 4-Hour Workweek.</u> New York, NY: Crown Publishers, 2007.

Franklin, Benjamin. <u>The Private Life of Benjamin Franklin.</u> London, England: Franklin, LL.D, 1793.

Hill, Napoleon. <u>Think and Grow Rich.</u> Hollywood, CA: Melvin Powers of Wilshire Book Company, 1937. (Current ISBN 1-59330-200-2)

Kanner, Bernice. <u>Pocketbook Power</u>. New York, NY: McGraw Hill, 2004.

Kocina, Lonny. <u>Media Hypnosis.</u> Minneapolis, MN: Mid-America Entertainment, Inc. 2002.

Power Stilson, Kim.   24 Hours to Zero Down Marketing.  Salt Lake City, UT. 2010.

Love, Lisa. Beyond the Secret.  Charlottesville, VA: Hampton Roads Publishing Company, 2007.

Lyon, Jack. Inspirational Classics. Salt Lake City, UT: Deseret Book Company, 2000.

Mandino, Og.   The Greatest Salesman in the World. New York, NY: Bantam Books, 1968

# APPENDIX

# TERMS

**Griefer** – a term which is most commonly used for online gamers who purposefully cause harm to gamers on and offline, yet it may also relate to folks who purposefully cause problems online.

**Blogosphere** -- meaning all blogs, it is an expression used to describe the 'world of blogs'.

**GUI** -- Pronounced **GOO**-ee according to Webpodedia is an acronym for graphical user interface or the graphics you see when you are on a website that leads you through the transactions.

**Infoedutainment© -- a combination of the words** information, education and entertainment coined by author Kim Power Stilson are meant to be a consumer content framework for series of creative content social media posts.

**Klog** -- not something stuck in your drain according to Webopedia, klog is short for the term Knowledge Blog and is used internally in companies to share technical content or corporate knowledge.

**Shoulder Surfing** -- Shoulder surfing refers to looking over another person's shoulder while they are in front of their computer screen, to obtain information. In some cases shoulder surfing is done for no reason other than to get an answer.

**Netiquette** -- The term "netiquette" is a take-off term suggesting there is proper social behavior for Internet interaction first used in 1988.

# RESOURCES

## "Surthrival Series for Home-based Business Success"

*Take this 5-step training series so you can make money from home in the 21ˢᵗ Century!*

**Step ONE: Strategy!**

Create a marketing strategy & structure for your business in 24 Hours!

(Volume 1) "24 Hours to Zero Down Marketing Strategy"

(Volume 2) "24ZDM Hourly Workbook"

**Step TWO: Tools!**

Learn how to use Social and eMedia on the twenty-first-century Grapevine to feed and fund your family.

(Volume 3) "Grapevine Connection! Learn how savvy families use Social Media on the 21ˢᵗ Century Grapevine to feed and fund their families.

(Volume 4) "Learn to Blog, Ping, Pod, Stream, Bookmark, Blast, Release, Wiki, Widget, Web,

Link, Avatar, Tag, RSS, Twitter, Google & Bing, Globalpreneur, Smartphone, Skype, Pinterest, Instagram, Hulu & YouTube!"

## Step THREE: 24/7 Sales!

Connect and Sell to your Customers 24/7 Online while you play with the kids and grandkids!

(Volume 5) "Setting up Shop Online!"

(Volume 6) "Ready to Sell 2.0? Take ACTION with the 24 Hour Challenge!!"

(Volume 7) "Ready to Sell 2.0?" Workbook

## Step FOUR: Freedom!

Enjoy the virtual success and freedom of a Hostage Proof Website!

This course gives you step by step training teaching you to easily maintain, manage and create your own Website.

(Volume 8) "Own your own Hostage Proof Website!"

## Step FIVE: Talk!

Make global social connections and promote your business with Talk Radio!

(Volume 9) "Talking to your Customers = Dollars! Put a Voice & Face on your Website!!"

(Volume 10) "Launch Your Business"

(Volume 11) "Talk Show Host Training"

(Volume 12) "Surthrival Terms"

*eMedia and live class room training available on choosesurthrival.com